Simply Vegetarian

THE VEGETARIAN SOCIETY OF IRELAND was established in 1978, and has published this book answer to the many requests it receives from people who want information on vegetarianism. The l authors, Tracy Culleton and Dee Higgs, have been vegetarian for many years, and are active members Society.

'The animals of the world exist for their own reasons.
They were not made for humans
any more than black people were made for whites
or women for men.'

Alice Walker, writer, born 9 February 1944

Simply Vegetarian

Tracy Culleton   Dee Higgs

WOLFHOUND PRESS

First Published in 1999 by Wolfhound Press
An Imprint of Merlin Publishing
16 Upper Pembroke Street, Dublin 2, Ireland
Tel: + 353 1 676 4373
Fax: + 353 1 676 4368
publishing@merlin.ie

Text © 1999, Tracy Culleton, Dee Higgs
Recipes © 1999 Vegetarian Society of Ireland, PO Box 3010, Dublin 4
Illustrations © 1999 Dee Higgs

This Second Edition printed 2004

First Edition ISBN 0-86327-717-9
Second Edition ISBN 0-86327-923-6

A catalogue record for this book is available from the British Library.

10 9 8 7 6 5 4 3 2 1

Cover Illustration & Design by Eva Byrne
Typeset by Wolfhound Press
Printed in Sweden by ScandBook AB

Contents

Acknowledgements

Tracy Culleton, Dee Higgs andthe members of the committee of the Vegetarian Society of Ireland wish to express their thanks to the following people who helped during the various stages of the production of this book:

Betty Reeves for proofreading and doing a variety of other laborious but necessary tasks.

Russell Higgs and Petter Harris for proofreading and computer advice.

Síle Reeves, Patricia Timoney and Paul O'Hare for proofreading.

Deirdre Kuntz (VSI-approved cookery demonstrator) for her recipes.

Ita West (regular contributor to *The Irish Vegetarian magazine*) for her recipes.

And our thanks to all members, past and presen, who have helped to forward the cause of vegetarianism either within or outside the committee. In particular:

Christopher Fettes, Christy Stapleton, the late Moira Henry, Jackie Perry, Gerry Boland, George Reeves, Ruarc Gahan, Catherine Morrow, Carol McEnroe, Tim Cookson, Nicholas McMurry, David McCullagh, Fionnuala Murray, Maria Connolly, Stephen West and the Dublin Food Co-op.

Introduction

'Being vegetarian is like walking to Moscow.'

What?

This was during the BSE crisis, and I was talking to a very nice man on the freephone number that had been set up. He introduced the subject of vegetarianism (I hadn't told him I was vegetarian).

'Oh yes,' he went on. 'If you want to go to Moscow, there are two ways of getting there. You can walk, or you can fly. Obviously you'll get there both ways, but flying is much quicker and more direct. Being vegetarian is like walking to Moscow — it requires a lot more planning of what you'll eat to make sure you get the correct nutrients.' He went on to imply that vegetarians spent their every waking minute planning their diet to make sure they got the right nutrients.

If vegetarianism is like walking to Moscow, then it's with seven-league boots! Vegetarian nutrition is very simple. You do have to know what you're doing (but then, so do meat-eaters), but the 'rules' are not at all complicated.

In fact, this book can tell you in one sentence how to eat well on a vegetarian diet! (See p. 19.)

But *Simply Vegetarian* is much more than that. Of course we explain vegetarian nutrition so you'll know you're doing it right, but we also give you some of the reasons to be vegetarian, and show you the many advantages of vegetarianism. And last, but not least, we provide some delicious, easy and healthy recipes.

What is Vegetarianism?

A vegetarian diet excludes products that involve the killing of an animal — namely, *all meat, poultry and fish, and all derivatives of these, such as gelatine and lard.* Vegetarians do eat dairy products and eggs. However, only free-range eggs are considered within the vegetarian ethic, given the cruelty and suffering involved in battery egg farming. Also, in practice, an ideal vegetarian diet includes only a small amount of dairy products — these should be a supplement to, and not a staple of, the diet, as is explained further in the chapter on nutrition (see p. 15).

A vegan diet excludes all animal products. In addition to meat, poultry and fish, vegans eliminate from their diet *dairy products, eggs, honey and derivatives of these.*

If you are a new vegetarian, you will already have your reasons. But the arguments that follow may help you to clarify your reasons, so that you'll be able to defend your choice against the (sometimes aggressive) questions you will inevitably be asked. You may also discover some reasons that hadn't occurred to you.

Animal Welfare

Full details of modern farming methods are outside the scope of this book, but our bibliography (p. 136) should be of use if you are interested in learning more. In short, the breeding, rearing, transporting and slaughtering of so-called food animals are inevitably accompanied by much suffering and cruelty. But within any situation, accidents happen, short-cuts are taken, systems aren't perfect. Even if suffering were the exception, there could be no justification for risking this pain simply for human gratification. If humans needed meat to live, it could be justified, but we don't. The fact that vegetarians don't just fade away and die is ample proof of this.

It is sometimes argued that humans are naturally carnivorous: 'We are meant to eat meat; we have always eaten meat'. In fact, humans are not naturally carnivorous. Biologically we have more in common with herbivores. We have only vestigial canine teeth (no use for tearing meat), and we have broad molars for grinding plant foods. We have long colons like herbivores, rather than short ones like meat-eaters; we sweat through our skin like herbivores, rather than panting like carnivores; and while carnivores manufacture vitamin C internally (as there is no vitamin C in meat), herbivores cannot, and humans cannot.

It's funny how proponents of this 'we have always eaten meat' argument seem happy to abandon other customs of our forefathers, such as living in caves without central heating, medicine, or television. In fact, meat-eating probably began as a 'desperate measures for desperate times' solution to a dwindling food supply caused by climatic changes. As Desmond Morris, in his book *The Naked Ape*, says: 'We were driven to become flesh-eaters only by environmental circumstances, and now that we have the environment under control [...] we might be expected to return to our ancient primate feeding patterns.'

World Food Problems

Meat production is very wasteful of fertile land. By feeding crops to animals instead of directly to humans we lose up to 90 per cent of the protein. Put another way, it takes 10 kg (or 10lb) of plant protein fed to a cow for every 1 kg (or 1lb) of beef produced. (Hence the idea of recycling the animals by feeding them meat and bone meal, and we all know how that one worked out!)

A lot of food fed to animals is food that people can, and do, eat directly, such as grains and soya beans. Some of these foods are imported from the Third World, to be fed to our animals. A change to vegetarianism would vastly increase the amount of food available in a hungry world. Developing World problems are more complicated than this, but whereas as individuals we can't make the World Bank write off loans to the Third World, we can refuse to be part of a system that contributes to the hunger of others.

Environment

Animal husbandry causes great destruction to our environment. In South America, the rain forest is being destroyed to provide grazing land for meat production. (To produce one hamburger, an average of 5 square metres — 55 square feet — of rain forest are destroyed to provide the necessary grazing land for cattle.) Also, farm animals produce the second largest amount of methane — after wetlands — which contributes to the greenhouse effect.

Even in Ireland we have to cope with the tons of animal waste produced each year, and can experience water shortages that would be alleviated if we didn't have to give water to millions of animals to drink, and use it to wash away both their excrement and the abattoir filth (and we have all heard of rivers being polluted by 'slurry'). Beef is by far the most expensive food in terms of water usage. It takes 11,200 litres (2,464 gallons) of water to produce 450g (1lb) of beef. By contrast, it takes only 2,182 litres (480 gallons) per 450g (1lb) of soya beans, and 1,141 litres (251 gallons) per 450g (1lb) of brown rice. It has been estimated that 18,184 litres (4,000 gallons) of water are needed daily to provide the food of a meat-eater; a vegetarian needs 5,455 litres (1,200 gallons), and a vegan 1,364 litres (300 gallons). Here in Ireland water shortages mean not being able to wash your car or water your lawn; elsewhere they are far more serious.

Meat production also uses a lot of oil and petroleum — for example, heating farming units, transporting foodstuffs for animals, transporting animals to the abattoir, delivering meat to the consumer. Vegetarianism would help to preserve our diminishing stocks of oil, as well as reducing air pollution.

Personal Health

People often worry that a vegetarian diet is a risky one in terms of health. In fact, a vegetarian diet is not only as healthy as a meat-based one — it is far healthier.

There are no figures for Ireland, but figures from Britain show that vegetarians spend only 65 per cent of the time in hospital that meat-eaters do. And since we can assume that vegetarians have as many accidents, and get pregnant as often, the percentage of vegetarians in hospital because of illness must actually be lower still.

It is widely recognised by bodies such as the World Health Organisation and the Irish Department of Health that we should be eating less fat — especially saturated fat — and more fibre. A sensible vegetarian diet obviously achieves both of these aims.

Many studies have shown that a vegetarian diet actually protects against diseases such as heart disease and cancer, as well as other common so-called Western diseases. The list below gives further details.

Heart Disease (cardiovascular disease)

This is associated with diets high in fat, especially saturated fats — which means (with the exception of cocoa, coconut and palm oils) animal fat. Ireland's very high rate of death from heart disease is not surprising given our high intake of meat and dairy products. Many studies have shown that vegetarians are between 30 and 40 per cent less at risk of heart disease than are meat-eaters, even after factors such as smoking, drinking, exercise and environment are taken into account. The high iron intake of a traditional diet may also be to blame (see p. 17).

Cancers

One study estimated that about 35 per cent of all cancers are diet-related. Vegetarians suffer a much lower incidence of cancer of the colon, which is associated with a low-fibre diet, and vegetarian women have a lower incidence of breast cancer, which has been associated with a high-fat diet. In fact, it appears that vegetarians suffer lower incidences of all cancers, and research into this matter is ongoing.

One explanation is that vegetarians tend to eat more fruit and vegetables, and these plant foods contain the antioxidant vitamins A, C, and E, which help to protect against unavoidable toxins such as air pollution.

The authorities in Britain recently recommended that people who eat more than 90g of red meat a day should consider cutting down, and those who eat more than 140g daily should definitely cut down. While this does seem to be more red meat than most people eat, study after study shows that the more meat you eat, the greater your risk.

Osteoporosis

Vegetarian women suffer a significantly lower incidence of this disease (see p. 18 for details).

Obesity

The combination of high fibre and low fat means that vegetarians are less likely to be overweight. Obviously chips and ice-cream can be vegetarian, but a diet high in grains, beans, fruit and vegetables, with moderate amounts of nuts and dairy products, should prevent excess weight without resorting to diets.

Vegetarians also suffer much less from constipation and piles, which are associated with a low-fibre diet, and from gallstones, associated with a high-fat diet.

Food Poisoning

For most people food poisoning means a few days of sickness, but for others it can mean death. Meat and dairy products are responsible for the vast majority of food poisoning cases (E.coli, salmonella and listeria, for example).

Antibiotics

It is widely accepted that overuse of antibiotics is a major concern. Bacteria evolve incredibly quickly to develop resistance to antibiotics, and so the pharmaceutical industry is in a constant race against time to develop new antibiotics. This is very serious as, without antibiotics, even minor operations would be the hazardous enterprises that they once were, and illnesses like pneumonia would once again become life-threatening.

In relation to the argument for vegetarianism, the issue that concerns us is the regular use of antibiotics in farming. Because of the stress that farm animals are under, they can get sick easily, and their close physical proximity to one another means that illness spreads rapidly. Therefore, they are often given antibiotics. Humans ingest this antibiotic residue along with meat. There is a maximum permitted level of antibiotic residue, but a 1997 survey by the Consumer Association of Ireland found that 17 per cent of pork had higher than permitted levels.

Pesticide and Herbicides

If you are concerned about the residues of pesticides and fertilisers contained in vegetables, one answer is to eat organic (which we could all do, if we didn't have to provide so much food for animals). But since the foodstuffs which animals eat are also contaminated (and they eat 10 times as much per portion of meat), meat-eaters are eating even more of this than vegetarians are.

Why be Vegan?

If you are a new vegetarian, or are thinking about becoming vegetarian, don't panic. Veganism is something that tends to follow on from vegetarianism — very few people start off being vegan. If you are vegetarian, you are already greatly decreasing your contribution to the slaughter of animals, the destruction of the planet, the hunger of others, and your own ill-health — it's a big step, a step to be congratulated on. Don't feel that the text below is to pressure you into becoming vegan before you are ready. Or, worse, don't be put off being vegetarian because you think that if you can't go the whole hog (whoops, no pun intended!) there's no point in doing anything.

Having said that, there are compelling reasons for veganism.

Egg production is one of the most appalling examples of intensive farming. The birds are crowded together so tightly that as they rub off each other they abrade their feathers, causing pain. They tend to fight from stress, so their beaks are cut off. They have painful feet from standing on uncomfortable flooring, in their own excrement. They never see daylight. For all these reasons, the vegetarian movement has decided that battery-farmed eggs are totally beyond our ethics. So most vegetarians eat free-range eggs. However, there is still the problem of male birds being routinely killed at birth because they are of no commercial value, and the elderly female birds going to slaughter for meat. This is why vegans do not use any eggs.

Milk production is also very cruel. A cow has to be regularly put in calf so that she keeps producing milk every single day of her life. A cow will produce about ten times as much milk as she would naturally produce for a calf, and her calves will be removed at a few days old, to be raised either in their own turn as dairy cows, or for meat. When a cow is exhausted from these demands on her body, she'll be slaughtered for meat.

Vegetarian Nutrition

The list below shows the nutrients provided by meat. It combines the information in two leaflets: 'The Role of Meat in a Balanced Diet' (An Bord Bia), and 'Lean Meat' (CBF — Irish Livestock and Meat Board).

- Energy
- Protein
- Vitamin A
- Vitamins B1, B2, niacin, B6
- Vitamin B12
- Iron
- Zinc
- Phosphorus

All of these can easily be obtained from a vegetarian diet.

Energy

For meat to provide energy, the protein has to be converted to carbohydrate. A vegetarian diet is already rich in carbohydrates.

Protein

According to An Bord Bia, 'meat is the most important source of protein [in the Irish diet], accounting for some 34 per cent of protein intake'. However, this means that in a typical meat-eater's diet, the other 66 per cent is already coming from vegetarian sources. It is extremely easy to replace the 34 per cent with specifically high-protein vegetarian foods.

Vegetarians get protein from four main sources:

- *Nuts and Seeds*: e.g. almonds, cashews, walnuts, hazelnuts, peanuts, sesame seeds, sunflower seeds.
- *Beans and Lentils*: e.g. haricot beans (the traditional 'baked bean'), kidney beans, butter beans, red split lentils, brown lentils, green lentils, soya beans.
- *Wholefood Grains*: e.g. wheat, rice, millet, buckwheat, rye, barley, oats. Grains fall into two kinds: those with gluten (wheat, rye, barley, oats), and those without (rice, millet, buckwheat). Gluten is a protein, so even products made from white flour have some protein in them. The white versions of

other grains, such as rice, contain no nutrients other than carbohydrate/starch. However, the 'brown' bit of grains contains even more protein, as well as iron, fibre, and vitamins B and E. This is why wholefood grains are such a valuable part of the diet.

- *Eggs and Dairy Products*: e.g. free-range eggs, milk, yoghurt, cheese.

Proteins are made up of building blocks called amino acids. Eight of these together build one unit of protein. Meat and dairy products contain all eight amino acids, and used to be called 'first-class proteins'. The foods mentioned above do not (with the exception of soya beans — see Glossary), and were called 'second-class proteins'.

It was discovered that one type of vegetarian protein food (e.g. beans), was high in the amino acids in which another (e.g. grains) was low and vice versa. This led to the concept of 'protein combining'. By eating beans and grains together, you would have the required number of amino acids to make protein. Similarly with grains and nuts, beans and nuts, or any one of these with dairy products.

It has since been discovered that all foods except fruits contain some protein, and if you eat a reasonable amount of food, incorporating the four protein foodstuffs mentioned above, in as unprocessed a state as is possible, and eat a good variety of foods, you will get enough protein. You should also remember that an excess of protein can contribute to osteoporosis, as is further explained in the Calcium section on p. 18.

Vitamin A

There is an abundance of carotene in plant foods, which the body converts to vitamin A. (Carotene is sometimes called 'pro-vitamin A'.) Vitamin A, along with vitamin C (found only in plant foods) and vitamin E (of which there is a tiny amount in liver, but none in any other meat), contain antioxidants which help protect against cancer.

Vitamins B1, B2, niacin (B3), B6

There are many sources for these vitamins, such as brewer's yeast, yeast extract, wholegrains, beans, nuts, dairy products, leafy green vegetables (see the list of vitamins and minerals on p. 20). Vegetarians do not have to worry about getting enough of these vitamins.

Vitamin B12

Our need for vitamin B12 is minuscule, amounting to about one-seventeenth the size of an aspirin tablet over a lifetime. However, it is an essential nutrient, a shortage of which can lead to pernicious anaemia. Vegetarians will get all they need from dairy products and eggs. Vegans have to be more careful. A lot of foods are fortified with vitamin B12, such as soya milk, breakfast cereals, yeast extract, and TVP (see Glossary). If you are vegan, simply plan to include foods that contain this vitamin. Some vegans make a point of stirring a teaspoon or so of yeast extract into every savoury casserole they make.

Iron

Iron is one of the main nutrients that people associate with meat. The Department of Health goes so far as to state categorically that 'women should eat red meat at least three times a week'. The rationale is that meat-sourced iron is 'more easily absorbed by the body' than plant-sourced iron. However, when the body needs more iron, it steps up its plant-sourced iron-absorption ability. When iron levels have reached their optimum again, it reduces this ability and the iron in your food will pass unabsorbed. The only times when you need extra iron are after an accident (even a minor one like cutting your finger), menstruation, or donation.

The iron from meat, on the other hand, is so easily absorbed that it bypasses the body's natural iron-balancing ability, and it is all absorbed. When this happens you can end up having too much iron. There is increasing evidence to link an excess of iron in the diet with increased risk of heart disease, cancer and a poorer response to infection. In fact, several studies show that a vegan or nearly vegan diet can actually regress heart disease, with the blockages in arteries diminishing in size.

Many studies have shown that, although vegetarians can be anaemic, they will be so in no higher a proportion than meat-eaters. In fact, a good number of these studies have even found that vegetarians had higher iron stores than the control meat-eating group!

Having said that, it is very important, especially for women and girls, to get enough iron. The main sources of iron in the vegetarian diet are: dried fruit, leafy green vegetables, wholegrains, beans, lentils, millet, molasses, parsley, and pumpkin seeds (and Guinness, Murphy's and Beamish, of course!) Iron is more easily absorbed if eaten with vitamin C, as often naturally happens in the vegetarian diet (meat, on the other hand, contains no vitamin C at all).

Getting your iron from food sources is preferable to popping pills, as your body can take what it needs, whereas with pills the body has to take what it's given.

Zinc

The sources of zinc in the vegetarian diet are sesame seeds, pumpkin seeds, cheese, almonds, wheat germ, beans, lentils, and wholegrains. Plant sources may be somewhat lower in available zinc than meat, but a plant-based diet also reduces zinc excretion. Studies have shown that zinc levels are fine on a vegetarian diet, and adaptation to lower intakes also seems to occur.

Phosphorus

Phosphorus is found in all vegetarian foods. Deficiency is unknown except in people being fed intravenously, and those suffering alcohol-related liver damage.

Calcium

There is no calcium in meat, but it is still an issue, as calcium tends to be equated with milk and other dairy products. In fact, humans are the only species to drink the milk of another species, or drink milk at all beyond infancy. About 10 per cent of Irish people are intolerant of, or fully allergic to, dairy products, and the figure is nearly 100 per cent for some other races.

Dairy products are high in saturated fat, and have no fibre, which is the exact opposite of the widely accepted healthy-eating guidelines (skimmed and semi-skimmed milk try to address the high-fat issue).

Vegetarian women suffer less osteoporosis than the general population of women although they eat only a small amount of dairy products, or even none at all. It is becoming increasingly clear that the important issues are not so much the amount of calcium you take in, as the amount you excrete, and how much *protein* you eat.

The body uses calcium to digest protein. So, the more protein you eat, the more calcium is needed to process it, and therefore the less calcium remains in your body. A typical meat-eater's diet is high in protein, and so uses a lot of calcium. Dairy products are also high in protein, so a lot of the calcium in them is used to process the protein. Animal protein seems to cause this calcium-leaching effect more than plant proteins.

Studies of populations such as the Chinese, who eat no dairy products, show that they have an extremely low rate of osteoporosis. Eskimos, who eat a diet extremely high in both protein and calcium (in the form of fish bones), have a high rate of osteoporosis. Laboratory studies have shown that the higher in protein the diet, the more calcium is excreted in urine.

Both boron and vitamin D are essential in enabling the body to use calcium. Boron is a mineral found only in plant foods. Vitamin D can be found in margarine and oils, and the best source of all is daylight. Sunshine on the skin synthesises into vitamin D, without any need for dietary additions. Even in an Irish winter, twenty or thirty minutes a day of daylight exposure to the face and hands is sufficient. And if you walk in the daylight for half an hour, you are also engaging in weight-bearing exercise, which is essential to preventing osteoporosis.

Plant foods rich in calcium include leafy green vegetables, beans, seeds (especially sesame seeds), almonds, molasses and seaweeds. It is worth getting into the habit of sprinkling sesame seeds onto all sorts of dishes — your breakfast cereal, the top of a nut roast, into bread dough, etc.

Many vegetarian foods, such as leafy green vegetables and pulses, contain both iron and calcium. If you include these foods regularly in your diet, you won't go wrong. In the Introduction, we mentioned that we could tell you how to eat well on a vegetarian diet in one sentence. Here's the (admittedly convoluted) sentence:

Base your diet around wholegrains, beans, lentils, fruit and vegetables (especially leafy green vegetables such as broccoli, sprouts, cabbage, kale, spinach, parsley), using nuts and seeds in moderation (almonds and walnuts are excellent), and dairy products in moderation (if at all), making sure that you eat a good variety of food, and that it is as unprocessed as is reasonable in the real world.

Supplements

Some people say that even in a healthy, balanced diet, the food we eat is so far from the ground it grew in that its vitamin and mineral content is depleted. Others argue that we just don't need supplements, especially since some can be dangerous in excess. The Vegetarian Society of Ireland believes that vegetarians have no greater need for supplements than meat-eaters. However, there are a few exceptions.

Vitamin B12: Vegans might wish to take a supplement of vitamin B12.

Vitamin D: People with very dark complexions may not get enough of this vitamin from Irish sunshine, and should take a supplement, but only with qualified advice, as too much can be toxic.

Folic Acid: For women expecting to conceive, a supplement of folic acid is recommended. They should also be sure to include plenty of folic acid in their diets, both before conception and for the first three months of pregnancy. This will help protect against spina bifida in the baby.

Calcium: Excess calcium is excreted from the body, and therefore it is a safe supplement to take, if you feel you would like the insurance it brings, especially if you eat only a small amount of dairy products, or none at all.

Vitamins and Minerals

This list is a summary of much of the information already given, and is by no means a complete list of all the sources of vitamins and minerals in vegetarian foods.

Vitamin A: Most fruit and vegetables (especially carrots, green leafy vegetables, peppers, broccoli), margarine, dried apricots, cheese, butter.

Vitamin B1 (thiamine): Dried brewer's yeast, yeast extract, wholegrains, nuts (especially peanuts, Brazil nuts, pistachio nuts, pecans), sunflower seeds, sesame seeds, fortified products such as breakfast cereals.

Vitamin B2 (riboflavin): Yeast extract, dairy products, millet, wholegrains, wholewheat pasta, mushrooms, almonds, leafy green vegetables, fruits, miso, quinoa, fortified products such as breakfast cereals.

Vitamin B3 (niacin): Yeast extract, peanuts, wholegrains, dried brewer's yeast, brown rice, fortified products such as breakfast cereals.

Vitamin B6: Wholegrains, bran, nuts, avocados, wheat germ, yams, brown rice flour, peanut butter, sesame seeds, chick-peas, sunflower seeds, fortified breakfast cereals.

Vitamin B12: Eggs, cheese, milk, fortified products such as yeast extract, textured vegetable protein, Ribena and breakfast cereals.

Folic acid: Yeast extract, soya flour, peanuts, raw spinach and cabbage, toasted wheat germ, sunflower seeds, mung beans, soy flour, fortified products such as breakfast cereals.

Vitamin C: Most green, red or orange fruit or vegetables, especially red and green peppers, blackcurrants, lemon juice, orange juice, kiwi fruit, citrus fruit and juice.

Vitamin D: Sunlight, eggs, cheese, margarine, fortified products.

Vitamin E: Wheat germ and wheat-germ oil, vegetable oils, margarine, nuts and nut oils, tahini, seeds, avocados, olives, dark green leafy vegetables.

Calcium: Cheese, milk (including soya milk), eggs, leafy green vegetables (including seaweeds), beans (especially soya beans, baked beans and kidney beans), sesame seeds and tahini, dried fruit, molasses, broccoli, carob powder.

Iron: Dried fruit, wholegrains, pulses, molasses, soya products including tofu, wheat germ, parsley, prunes, dates, dried apricots, pumpkin seeds, millet, green leafy vegetables, wholemeal bread, fortified breakfast cereals, sesame seeds.

Magnesium: Nuts (especially almonds, Brazil nuts, peanuts, walnuts, cashew nuts), green vegetables, dried fruits (especially prunes), soya beans, bananas, wholegrains, wheat germ, seeds, pulses, tofu, cheese, wholemeal bread and pasta, brown rice.

Zinc: Seeds (especially pumpkin seeds, sesame seeds), cheese, lentils, wholegrains, almonds, peanuts, walnuts, wheat germ, wheat bran, brewer's yeast, pulses, tofu, milk, bean sprouts, oatmeal, brown rice, wholegrain bread and pasta, miso.

Omega-3 fatty acids: An excellent source of these is linseeds (or linseed oil).

The Vegetarian Mother and Baby

Pregnancy

A vegetarian diet provides all the nutrients you need during pregnancy, just as it does at other times in your life. Below is a list of the major nutrients you require during pregnancy, and the vegetarian sources:

Protein: All foods, with the exception of fruit, contain some protein, and therefore extra protein will be obtained from the extra food you eat as your pregnancy advances and your appetite increases.

Iron: This is an extremely important nutrient, and your iron needs increase during pregnancy. Iron-rich foods include: wholegrain cereals, pulses (beans, peas and lentils), green vegetables and dried fruit. Blackstrap molasses is a very rich source of iron, although its strong taste won't appeal to everyone. As your iron needs grow, your body increases its efficiency at extracting iron from plant foods, so once you include these foods in your diet you should be getting plenty of iron.

Calcium: Dairy products, especially cheese, are the most obvious source. However, there are many plant sources too. These include: pulses (especially soya beans), almonds, sesame seeds (and tahini, which is creamed sesame seeds and comes in a jar), dried fruit, green vegetables, carob powder and molasses.

B vitamins: These are also very important. The best source is brewer's yeast, which is available from healthfood shops and can be mixed with just enough orange juice to make it drinkable. It provides a large percentage of your daily B vitamin requirement, as well as extra iron. The only B vitamins for vegans to worry about are B2 (riboflavin) and B12. Sources of B2 include millet, wholewheat pasta, fortified breakfast cereals, leafy green vegetables and mushrooms. Dairy products are a significant source for non-vegans. If you eat dairy products you don't have to worry about B12. If you don't, we recommend that you take a supplement. Some vegetarian foods — such as TVP, breakfast cereals, and some soya milks — are fortified with vitamin B12.

Folate (folic acid): This is now known to be vital in preventing birth defects such as spina bifida. All women, vegetarian or not, are strongly advised to take a supplement whilst trying to conceive and for the first three months of pregnancy.

Vitamin D: The body needs vitamin D to use calcium properly. The best sources from diet are dairy products and margarine. Twenty minutes of daylight a day will give most Irish people enough vitamin D. If you are considering a supplement, get specific medical advice, as too much vitamin D can be toxic.

Zinc: This mineral is vital during pregnancy. Sources include wheat germ and wheat bran, nuts, bean sprouts, oatmeal, brown rice, cheese, sweetcorn, peas and milk.

Magnesium: Nuts, pulses, wholegrains and dried fruit are rich in magnesium. Fresh fruit and vegetables also contribute, particularly potatoes and bananas.

Iodine: The main source of iodine is seaweed. Vegetarians use seaweeds such as kelp, kombu or carrageen moss. If you enjoy the taste of seaweeds, you can sprinkle some on salads. If you don't like the taste, you can take kelp tablets instead.

In short, the following foods are good to base your diet around:

- Wholegrain cereals.
- Pulses, especially soya products and sprouted pulses (sprouted chick-peas are particularly tasty).

- Nuts and seeds, especially almonds and sesame seeds for calcium.
- Fresh fruit and vegetables, especially leafy green vegetables.
- Dried fruits.

You might also like to include some brewer's yeast, with a daily tablespoon of molasses and wheat germ. If you are vegan, a vitamin B12 supplement would be a good idea. Also include seaweeds as mentioned in the paragraph on Iodine.

Breastfeeding

You can breastfeed healthily on a vegetarian or a vegan diet. If you are breastfeeding, try to keep to a similar diet to that which you had during pregnancy. Any deficiencies in your diet will not affect your milk, as the milk production has first call on the nutrition the mother takes in, but what will happen is that *you* will lose out. The only exception is that if your diet is very lacking in fat, your milk may be low in fat.

In fact, as a vegetarian, your milk will actually be better than that of meat-eaters. According to John Robbins in *Diet for a New America*, 99 per cent of US mothers' milk contains significant levels of DDT, as against only 8 per cent of vegetarian mothers' milk.

Weaning

It's perfectly okay to raise a child on a vegetarian diet. There have been many studies undertaken, and they have all proven that vegetarian children grow up just as tall, just as intelligent, just as healthy as their meat-eating peers. In fact, just as for adults, a vegetarian diet is much healthier for children, helping to protect them against later heart disease, cancers, and other diseases.

The following recipe suggestions for babies simply require puréeing to a thick mixture for a very young baby, and gradually increasing the texture as the baby is more able for it. Although the quantities given in these recipes are small, you can batch-cook and freeze.

In these recipes you can use cow's milk, soya milk or breast-milk. Dairy and soya milk are not suitable for babies under a year to drink in large quantities, but using them in cooking is fine. The only exception is if there are dairy allergies in your family, in which case don't use dairy products until the baby is a year old.

Carrot 'n' Cheese
*You can use some of the carrot cooking water
to thin this dish down if you wish.*
2 tbsp cooked carrot
2 tbsp vegetarian cottage or cheddar cheese, grated

Creamed Corn
2 tbsp corn kernels, cooked
1 tbsp milk

Peas Please
2 tbsp cooked peas
2 tbsp milk
1 tbsp vegetarian cottage cheese

Tapiocanana
½ small banana
3 tbsp cooked tapioca
1 tbsp milk

Lentil Mash
50g/2oz cooked red lentils
50g/2oz cooked potato
1–2 tbsp milk

Don't give any foods containing gluten (wheat, oats, barley or rye) until the baby is at least six months old, and possibly for a time after that if you have allergies in your family. Lentils and beans can be introduced at about seven months. Tofu, mashed with some vegetable, is excellent food.

Babies shouldn't be given any food containing either salt or sugar — although this can be quite hard to achieve given outside influences and baby's own desires.

There is a small vegetarian range of babyfoods in jars (and some brands use organic ingredients). These are simply real food, cooked and puréed, and so are preferable to powdered packet foods.

An important thing to remember when feeding babies and children is that their stomachs are tiny, so they need to eat little and often. Snacks are the order of the day: brown bread and nut butter (peanut butter is the classic, but almond and cashew butters are also available from healthfood shops. Or you can make your own by very finely grinding nuts with some vegetable oil). Other snacks include apple or pear cubes, banana, pieces of cooked broccoli or peas, soya or dairy yoghurt. Be wary of raw carrot for a small child, as it can flake and cause choking, but lightly cooked carrot sticks are great. When your child is old enough, you can provide raw carrot sticks, cashews or dried fruit, but take care that the dried fruit is not too laxative.

There are three very important points with regard to bringing up vegetarian children.

Firstly, because children have higher nutritional needs than adults, they need more energy-dense food. This means that the 'high-fibre/low-fat' rule that adults should live by is practically reversed. Within reason, make sure that vegetarian children do not eat too much fibre and that they eat a good amount of fat.

Secondly, be careful to include lots of iron-rich food in your child's diet: beans, green vegetables, dried fruit and egg yolk are all good sources. One of the symptoms of iron deficiency is lethargy, so a child who is bounding around the place is probably getting enough iron.

Thirdly, vegetarian children mature more slowly than meat-eating children. This has positive benefits, but don't be surprised if your vegetarian child is shorter than average during childhood. Many studies have shown that vegetarian children end up the same average height as meat-eaters. High-protein diets bring quick growth but equally quick degeneration, whilst low-protein diets bring slower growth but also slower degeneration. Vegetarian children also undergo puberty at a later stage than meat-eaters, and this can have very good benefits. For example, early onset of menstruation has been linked with a higher risk of later ovarian and breast cancer.

Anorexia and Vegetarianism

There is no doubt that there can be some link between vegetarianism and anorexia, especially in teenage girls. But it is very important to note that vegetarianism does not cause anorexia.

However, for an anorexic teenager, vegetarianism provides an ideal excuse to move away from the family diet. Since a change to vegetarianism can often cause weight loss (to a stable, healthy weight), an excessive weight loss might not be immediately noticed.

Vegetarianism does not mean just vegetables, so eating only vegetables is not a proper vegetarian diet. The vegetarian basic foodstuffs such as nuts, seeds, beans, lentils and grains are all high-carbohydrate, reasonably stodgy foods, and if someone is happily eating these, there is no problem. As with any diet, the amount someone eats will also be an indication.

Fear of anorexia is no reason to forbid a teenager to go vegetarian. That would be like forbidding someone to cross bridges because some people jump off them. A proper, fairly balanced diet helps protect against many diseases, and is a very positive step for anyone to take. However, as some anorexic teenagers might use vegetarianism as a ploy, parents should watch for it and take early steps if necessary.

The reality is that although a lot of anorexics call themselves vegetarian, very few vegetarians are anorexic.

Animal Products

Being a strict vegetarian is much more than not eating meat. Listed below are by-products of the slaughter-house, and other animal ingredients used where you mightn't expect them. It is important to be aware that manufacturers change their ingredients. For example, Stork margarine was vegetarian until the manufacturers began to use fish oils in it. They have since dropped this ingredient (at the time of going to print). Look out for the VSI and VSUK symbols — your guarantee that there are no animal products in the ingredients.

Anchovies

These fish are usually listed as an ingredient in Worcester-shire sauce. Goodall's brand is free of anchovies (at the time of going to print). Shoyu is a very good alternative.

Battery Hen Eggs

These are not compatible with the vegetarian ethic because of the horrendous cruelty inherent in their production. You can assume that eggs used in bought products, such as quiches, will be from battery sources.

Cochineal (also listed as carmine or E120)

This red food colouring is made from ground-up beetles.

Fish Oil (also called marine oil)

This is found in some block margarines, and also in baked products such as cakes and biscuits.

Gelatine

This is made from boiled-up bones, hooves and other bits of animals left over after slaughter. It is regularly used in all sorts of foods, such as jellies, sweets, cheesecakes, mints, cakes, desserts and low-fat yoghurts. There is a vegetarian gelling agent, called Vege-gel, which is excellent, and is made from seaweed.

Lard

Lard is animal fat, and is found in some cakes, biscuits and pastries. Butter or vegetarian or vegan margarine are good substitutes for home baking. Check that shortening or fat used in shop-bought products is of vegetable origin.

Meat Stock (usually beef or chicken)

This can be found in some tinned and packet soups and sauces, and is often used in restaurant soups.

Rennet

Traditionally, hard cheeses such as cheddar were set using rennet, which is taken from the lining of calves' stomachs. Cheeses marked as being vegetarian use a microbial rennet. Soft cheeses such as cottage cheese usually do not contain rennet, but check before buying. Many farmhouse cheeses are vegetarian, even if they are not marked as such — ask the manufacturer or retailer.

Suet

This fat from around the kidneys of the animal is traditionally used in Christmas puddings and mincemeat. For home baking, use vegetarian suet or margarine in puddings and simply leave it out of mincemeat — there is no difference in taste.

Glossary

The following foods are used frequently in most vegetarian diets. Many are based on soya beans, which are super-nutritious, being high in protein (they contain all the essential amino acids), fibre, vitamins and minerals. Soya beans are higher in fat than other beans (which have negligible fat), but are still low-fat compared with other foods. There is some evidence, not yet conclusive, that women who eat a lot of soya products suffer a lower incidence of breast, ovarian and uterine cancer — perhaps because soya beans contain a substance similar to the female hormone oestrogen.

Carob

Carob is often used in the vegetarian diet in place of cocoa products. It contains no caffeine, is lower in fat, is naturally sweeter so needs less added sugar, and it contains more vitamins and minerals than cocoa. Cocoa also contains substances that inhibit the absorption of calcium (although chocolate manufacturers may extol the amount of milk in their products), whereas carob does not. It comes in bars or drops, and is treated just like chocolate. Carob powder is used in the same way as cocoa powder. In baking there is no real difference in taste.

Carob beans are also called locust beans, and there is a theory that when Saint John the Baptist lived on 'honey and locusts' he was in fact eating carob beans. This gives rise to the name 'Saint John's bean', by which carob is also known.

Miso

Miso is soya beans fermented together with a grain (you can get rice miso, barley miso or wheat miso). It is a dark, savoury paste, which like shoyu adds a 'meaty' taste to food. It is a good source of vitamin B12, although there is some doubt as to how well this B12 can be absorbed by the body. To cook with it, dissolve a little paste in cold water and add it to your dish at the end of cooking. Stir until it dissolves, but don't boil it as this destroys the nutrients. Like shoyu, miso is quite expensive, but you only need a small amount for a wonderful flavour.

Seaweeds

Seaweeds such as kelp, wakame, and nori are not found in most Irish cupboards. However, they are well worth incorporating into the vegetarian diet as they are an excellent source of iodine, and some seaweeds are rich in calcium. If you like the taste, you can include them in salads and soups. Otherwise, you can take kelp tablets (which are not a supplement, but food in tablet form).

Shoyu

Shoyu, also known as soya sauce or soy sauce, is another soya-bean product. A dark, salty liquid, very high in nutrients, it is usually associated with Oriental cookery, but is a valuable addition to many savoury dishes, providing a rich, 'meaty' taste. As it is quite salty, use less added salt when cooking with it. A bottle lasts a long time, and the better brands (we recommend Meridian and Kikkoman) are worth the extra expense. Avoid brands with ingredients such as 'extract of soya bean' or 'caramel'.

Soya Milk

Soya milk, made from soya beans, comes in tetra-paks, and is more expensive than cows' milk. It keeps for a long time while sealed, and for about three to four days once opened. It is good in milkshakes, with cereal, for white sauces, and in soups. However, it can curdle when added to hot liquids such as tea or coffee (this does not affect the taste, only the appearance). One way of avoiding this is to add the milk first, then stir the drink continuously as the hot liquid is added.

Soya milk is very high in protein, and contains about the same calories and fat content as semi-skimmed dairy milk. Some brands have added vitamins such as A and D, and added calcium. Soya milk is not suitable for infants but is fine for older children.

Stocks

There are several good brands, but we suggest that you read the ingredients carefully and buy brands that contain only vegetables. Those with monosodium glutamate and salt high up on the list of ingredients are not recommended. Vegetable cooking water and bean cooking liquid both make very good stocks.

Tahini

Tahini is made from creamed sesame seeds, and is like peanut butter made with sesame seeds. A high-fat food, it is also extremely high in calcium, and well worth incorporating in your diet. It is a key ingredient in hummus (recipe on p. 115), and can be stirred into a nut roast mixture to help bind it, and to add extra nutrients. We recommend light tahini for your first taste, as the dark version might be too strong tasting.

Tamari

Tamari is like shoyu and the two can be used interchangeably. The advantage to tamari is that it contains no grain products, and so is suitable for coeliacs.

Tofu

Tofu, also known as bean curd, is basically cheese made from soya milk. It comes in creamy-white blocks and is an extremely high-protein, low-fat food. Its bland taste lends itself well to all sorts of flavourings, both sweet and savoury. It is available in three densities: firm, soft and silken. The silken tofu, which comes in tetra-paks, is much more expensive than the firm tofu, which is sold in blocks. Although most cookbooks recommend that you use only silken tofu in such things as 'milk'-shakes, it is our experience that the firm tofu is fine for all uses, as long as it is blended well.

Tofu can be difficult to buy and will keep for only about a week in a fridge, covered in water that is changed daily. It can be frozen, but upon thawing has a spongy texture which is fine for casseroles and stir-fries, but not for shakes or sweet dishes. Despite these limitations, it is well worth experimenting with. Tofu processed with reconstituted apricots makes a highly nutritious fruit fool or baby food. Blended with a banana, a drop or two of vanilla essence and some soya milk, it makes a lovely, nutritious shake.

TVP

TVP — Textured Vegetable Protein— is 'mock meat', made from de-fatted soya bean flour, and is a high-protein, low-fat food. As a stand-by and occasional meal, it's great, but it is quite processed. The dried variety is available in chunks or mince, in plain or 'beef' flavours. The 'beef' flavouring comes from yeast extract, so the flavoured version is also high in B vitamins. It comes dehydrated and keeps very well. To use, simply cover in plenty of boiling water and leave to reconstitute for ten to fifteen minutes — it will double in size as it absorbs the water. It is then ready to use. When using as a meat substitute in traditional meat dishes, add it with your liquid — don't fry it as you would with mincemeat. 'Beef' TVP mince is lovely in shepherd's pie.

TVP can be bought in healthfood shops and in some supermarkets. Being processed, it is more expensive than beans and grains, but still cheap compared to meat, especially as it doubles in size, and there is no wastage.

Yeast Extract

Yeast extract (such as Marmite) is wonderfully nutritious. It is very high in B vitamins, especially vitamin B12, and is worth using regularly. Wholemeal toast spread with yeast extract is a very nutritious snack, and a teaspoon or two can be stirred into casseroles for added flavour and nutrition.

Notes on the Recipes

Vegetarian cookery is not complicated. You don't have to be too precise about measurements, and you don't need to worry about the positioning of ingredients in the fridge. One thing you will probably need is a food processor (not necessarily an expensive model). It is perfect for chopping nuts and vegetables, making pâtés and blending soups. The recipes here will act as springboards to ideas of your own. Don't be afraid to experiment.

Some people prefer to plan their meals around the familiar shapes of a traditional main course (such as burger or nut roast), with potatoes and vegetables, or stews. Others are happy to have no rules, eating as the Indians do, with two or three dishes, and rice, but no dish that could be called the 'main' one. Some of the recipes in the Starters and Accompaniments chapters of this book would also make excellent lunches.

Freezing Food

Most of the recipes included here freeze very well, so if you're organised, you can batch-cook and freeze dishes.

Recipes marked 'f' keep well in the freezer.

Vegan Recipes

A good replacement for beaten egg is chick-pea flour, also known as gram flour or besan flour. Using a fork, simply mix together one tablespoon of chick-pea flour to every two tablespoons of water. When it is mixed to the consistency of thin beaten egg, it can be used to coat burgers before dipping them in breadcrumbs. Chick-pea flour is preferable to free-range eggs because it involves no animal products, has no cholesterol, and is cheaper.

Recipes marked 'v' are vegan, or can be adapted. To do this, you exclude or replace the following ingredients:

- *Margarine*: use vegan margarine.
- *Butter*: substitute vegan margarine.
- *Honey*: substitute golden syrup or maple syrup.
- *Milk*: use soya milk.
- *Cream*: use soya milk.
- *Cheese*: omit.
- *Wine and sherry*: these are rarely vegan, so omit the alcohol from the recipes containing them.

Recipes listing the following ingredients cannot be vegan:

- *Eggs*: these are a necessary part of all the recipes which include them, and cannot be omitted.

- *Cheese*: in the recipes not marked with a 'v', the cheese is an integral part and cannot be omitted.

Onions and Garlic

Most vegetarian dishes seem to start with 'fry an onion and garlic'. A brilliant time-saver is to peel a whole net of onions and one or two bulbs of garlic (microwaving a bulb for about thirty seconds on a medium heat will make it easier to peel). Chop them in a food processor, then fry. Place portions of the fried mixture on a tray — an ice-cream scoop is ideal for this — and freeze. When the onions are solid, put them into a freezer bag. Although reasonably time-consuming when you do it, it means getting the knife and chopping board out only once, and because you are chopping so many onions it's worthwhile using the food processor. It also saves ten minutes' cooking time with each dish.

When using in soups or casseroles, add the frozen ball to the saucepan with the other ingredients, and cook following the recipe instructions. To use it in a nut roast, defrost it first. Because frozen garlic can lose its flavour after a couple of weeks, make this a high-turnover item in your freezer.

Cooking Dried Pulses

Before cooking beans, peas and lentils, remove stones and grit, then rinse well. Soak in plenty of cold water for about eight hours (overnight is ideal). Lentils and black-eyed beans do not need soaking. Pulses double their volume in soaking, so make sure that the container is big enough and that there is plenty of water. This doubling in size makes pulses, which are already cheap to buy, an incredibly inexpensive source of protein.

After soaking, drain and rinse in fresh water. Place in a large saucepan with plenty of water. Do not add salt as this toughens the skins and delays cooking. Bring to the boil. You may have to remove some surface scum, but it is not dangerous and does not taste bad. **Red and black kidney beans should be fast-boiled for at least ten minutes to kill off dangerous toxins.** When the pulses have come to the boil, or the kidney beans have boiled for ten minutes, lower the heat and simmer uncovered until soft but not mushy. Cooking time varies depending on the age of the pulses and the soaking time. Use the table opposite as a rough guide and keep testing. Top up the saucepan with boiling water as required. When the pulses are cooked, drain them, but keep the cooking liquid for rich, tasty, nutritious stock.

Beans can be cooked very successfully in the pressure cooker, taking about one-third as long as with beans you can cook at one time, you might prefer to cook in the normal way and freeze what you don't use.

Cooking Times for Pulses

Bean/Pea/Lentil	Cooking Time
Aduki beans	40 minutes
Black-eyed beans	45 minutes
Butter beans	45 minutes
Flageolet beans	1 hour
Haricot beans	45 minutes
Kidney beans	1 hour (including 10 mins boiling)
Lima beans	45 minutes
Mung beans	40 minutes
Pinto beans	1 hour
Soya beans	2 hours
Chick-peas	1½–2 hours
Marrowfat peas	1½ hours
Split peas	45 minutes
Brown lentils	30–40 minutes
Green lentils	30–40 minutes
Split red lentils	20 minutes

To Sprout Pulses

Pulses increase dramatically both in volume and nutrition when they are sprouted (as do grains and seeds). All pulses, with the exception of kidney beans and split red lentils, can be sprouted.

Soak the pulses overnight or all day. Sift through them, removing any damaged ones as these won't grow and could rot and spoil the others. Put the pulses into a large, clean jam or coffee jar. Cover with muslin, or an old segment of (clean!) tights or a J-cloth. Secure the covering with an elastic band. At least twice a day, fill the jar with water, through the cloth, to wet the pulses, and swirl the pulses around in the water. Then turn the jar upside down and drain it very well (if they aren't well drained, they will rot). Ideally, the sprouting pulses should be kept somewhere warm and dark, such as the hot press. However, it may be more practical to keep them beside the kitchen sink in a relatively dark area (under the sink, perhaps, as long as they're well away from bleaches, disinfectants and other poisonous substances), where you can get at them easily for rinsing.

The sprouts will be ready in two to four days, after which you may like to leave them for a day in a sunny place to increase their chlorophyll content. You can eat them in salads, or as snacks, or stir-fry them lightly. They will keep for about another four days in a plastic bag in the fridge.

To Cook Grains

The best way to cook grains is by the 'absorption' method, which means carefully measuring the amount of water in which they are cooked. By the time the grains are cooked, all the water is absorbed, and no vitamin-rich water remains to be thrown away.

The ratio of water to grains is as follows:

Rice, buckwheat and millet	2 units of water per unit of grain
Barley and wheat	3 units of water per unit of grain

(A unit refers to a volumetric unit, and can be a cup, a fluid ounce, a litre, etc.)

Wash and rinse the chosen grain, then put it into a saucepan with a little salt. Add the measured water, cover the pan and bring to the boil. When the water starts to boil, turn the heat to the lowest possible setting and leave to cook for the required time as indicated below. Although you can lift the lid from time to time to check, be sure to leave it on to preserve most of the steam. Do not stir the grain. Because of its wholemeal covering, it will keep its shape and not disintegrate into mush.

The cooking times for grains are (approximately) as follows:

Cooking Times for Grains

Grain	Cooking Time
Barley	50–60 minutes
Bulgar wheat	10 minutes*
Millet	20–25 minutes
Rice	30–40 minutes
Wheat	60 minutes

* Bulgar wheat can also be cooked by pouring boiling water over it and leaving to stand for 20 minutes.

Grains can also be cooked successfully in either the pressure cooker or the microwave (refer to the manufacturer's book for details). Cooking in the microwave will not save any time, but you can cook it in the serving dish and save on washing up.

Grains double in weight and volume during cooking because of the absorbed water, making them even more economical than they appear at first sight.

For a different taste you can sauté the grains (in spices, if desired) before adding the water. This adds to the flavour, but also to the calories. Alternatively, try cooking them in stock rather than plain water, or replace some water with wine, or add saffron.

Wholegrains may be sprouted in the same way as pulses, and this dramatically increases their vitamin and mineral content.

Wholegrains will keep for about six months in dark, airtight conditions. Processed grains can go rancid quickly because of their oil content, and will keep for approximately three months.

Points to Note

- Ovens vary, so cooking times vary. Most recipes will give a range of cooking times such as 10–15 minutes.
- All the recipes in this book serve four people unless otherwise stated.
- Spoon measurements are level unless otherwise stated.
- Egg sizes are not important, unless a size is specified.
- Use medium or large onions unless otherwise stated.
- Use margarine that is either vegetarian or vegan.
- For yeast extract, you can use either Marmite or Vecon. Both are quite salty, so add salt sparingly.
- We have specified scrubbing potatoes. This is worth doing, as much of the vitamin and mineral content is just under the skin. You can peel them if you prefer.

- If you have them, use fresh herbs as opposed to the dried ones specified. Parsley is much nicer fresh. It contains iron and calcium, and is very easy to grow. Use twice the quantity of fresh herbs as dried.
- For cooked beans or lentils, the weight specified is the cooked weight (about double the dried weight).
- Most recipes specify olive oil, as it is a very tasty and healthy oil. You can, however, use sunflower or another vegetable oil if you prefer.
- To grind nuts, use a food processor. A coffee grinder does an even better job, but you need to keep one specially for nuts as coffee would contaminate the taste.

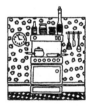

Tigers don't eat lettuce,
Men weren't meant for meat;
Monkeys, men or tigers —
We are what we eat.

Anonymous

Soups and Starters

Any of the following soups that contain cream can be adapted to a vegan dish if you use soya milk in place of the cream. All the soups, with the exception of the Apple and White Wine Soup, can be frozen if you want to make them in advance, but will freeze only without the cream or soya milk — add this when you are reheating to serve.

Ingredients

1 onion, peeled and finely chopped
1–2 cloves garlic, peeled and finely
    chopped
25g/1oz margarine or 2 tbsp olive oil
900g/2lb parsnips
1 tbsp curry powder
1.15 litres/2 pints vegetable stock
salt and pepper to taste
150ml/5fl oz cream or soya milk

Ingredients

1 onion, peeled and finely chopped
2 tbsp vegetable oil
450g/1lb fresh or tinned tomatoes,
    chopped
1 small carrot, scrubbed and grated
pinch of brown sugar
salt and pepper
850ml/30fl oz vegetable stock
75ml/3fl oz sour cream (optional)

Curried Parsnip Soup   vf

Gently fry the onion and garlic in the margarine or oil for about 10 minutes. While they are frying, prepare the parsnips — either scrub well or peel thinly. Cut into thick slices and leave to one side.

When the onions and garlic are soft, add the curry powder and fry for about 1 minute. Add the parsnips and the stock and bring to the boil. Lower the heat and simmer until the parsnips are tender (approximately 15–20 minutes). Season to taste, then purée well in a blender and add the cream. Reheat gently.

Tomato Soup   vf

Fry the onion in the oil until crisp and brown. Add the tomatoes, carrot, sugar and seasoning, and simmer for 5 minutes. Liquidise the mixture, then return to the pan. Add the stock and bring to the boil, stirring occasionally.

If you are using the sour cream, add a swirl on the top of each portion just before serving.

Carrot and Ginger Soup with Sesame Toast vf

The 'f' symbol refers to the soup, as long as you don't add the cream. However, the sesame toast does not freeze — make it when you need it.

Sauté the onions gently in the butter for approximately 5 minutes, then add the potatoes, carrots, ginger, and garlic. Stir together and cook gently, with the pan covered, for another 5 minutes. Add the water or stock and bring to the boil, then simmer for approximately 20 minutes, or until the carrots are tender. Liquidise the soup (or put it through a sieve), then add the lemon juice and season sparingly.

To make the sesame toast, grill each slice of bread on one side. Spread the untoasted sides with butter, and sprinkle generously with sesame seeds, pressing the seeds lightly into the bread with a spatula. Put the toast back under the grill until the butter has melted and the bread is golden brown and crispy. Cut into triangles.

The soup can be served either hot or chilled, with a swirl of cream on top if you are using this, and the coriander or parsley sprinkled over it.

Ingredients

2 large onions, peeled and finely chopped
25g/1oz butter
225g/8oz potatoes, scraped or peeled, and diced
700g/1½lb carrots, scraped or peeled, and diced
thimble-size piece of ginger, peeled and crushed
2 cloves garlic, peeled and crushed
1.15 litres/2 pints water or vegetable stock
2 tbsp lemon juice
salt and freshly ground black pepper to taste
150ml/5fl oz cream (optional)
fresh chopped coriander or parsley as garnish

For the Sesame Toast
4 slices wholemeal bread (or one for each person)
butter
sesame seeds

Ingredients

25g/1oz margarine
1 onion, peeled and finely chopped
1 leek, washed and sliced
salt and pepper
325–350g/12oz sweetcorn or cooked
    corn from 4 cobs
2 medium potatoes, scrubbed and cut
    into small cubes
275–300ml/10fl oz vegetable stock
575–600ml/1pint milk or soya milk

Ingredients

450g/1lb cooking apples, peeled,
    cored and cut into small pieces
575–600ml/1 pint water
275–300ml/10fl oz medium–dry white
    wine
demerara sugar to taste
ground cinnamon
ground nutmeg

Sweetcorn Chowder vf

Melt the margarine in a large, heavy saucepan. Add the onion and sauté for a few minutes. Add the leek, salt and pepper, and sauté for a few minutes more. Then add the corn and potatoes and mix well. Pour the vegetable stock and the milk over the mixture, stir, and bring to the boil. Simmer uncovered for 20 minutes.

Process the mixture until smooth, then reheat gently. Add some more water if you think the soup is too thick.

Apple and White Wine Soup

This very unusual soup, which is ideal for a summer dinner party, doesn't freeze well, but you can make it up to a day beforehand and keep it in the fridge until you are ready. It can be served hot or chilled.

Simmer the apples in the water until they are tender — about 10 minutes. Add the wine and the sugar, stirring until the sugar has dissolved. Liquidise the soup. Return to the saucepan and reheat to serve. Sprinkle with cinnamon and nutmeg before serving.

Onion Soup   vf

Traditional onion soup uses beef stock. For our version we use very well-flavoured stock by incorporating soya sauce and yeast extract. Tradition also has the soup served with toasted bread at the bottom of the bowl, as below. If you don't like this idea, simply leave it out and serve the soup with plenty of bread. To make a vegan version omit the cheese.

Melt the margarine in a large pan and fry the onions on a very low heat for about 15 minutes — this brings out their sweetness. Mix in the flour, stirring. Cook for a few seconds, then add the stock, soya sauce, yeast extract and the salt and pepper. Bring to the boil, then simmer gently for 30 minutes.

Just before you're ready to serve, grill the French bread slices on one side until they're toasted, then turn them over, sprinkle with the cheese (if using), and grill until the cheese is melted.

To serve, place a piece of the cheesy toast in the bottom of each bowl, and ladle the soup over it. Serve with the rest of the French stick.

Ingredients

25g/1oz margarine
700g/1½lb onions, peeled and finely sliced
15g/½oz flour
850ml/30fl oz vegetable stock or water
½ tsp soya sauce
½ tsp yeast extract
salt and pepper
50g/2oz vegetarian cheddar cheese, grated (optional)
1 slice of French bread per person

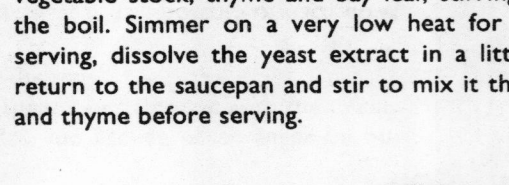

Ingredients

1 onion, peeled and chopped
2 large carrots, scrubbed and sliced
2 stalks celery, washed and sliced
2 tbsp vegetable oil
2 tbsp fine oatmeal
850ml/30fl oz vegetable stock or
    water
1 sprig thyme
1 bay leaf
1 tsp yeast extract

This traditional soup can be served with some soda bread or batch loaf. You can add some scrubbed and chopped potatoes if you want to make it more substantial.

Fry the onion, carrot and celery in the oil for between 5 and 10 minutes. Add the oatmeal and stir for 1 minute more. Add the vegetable stock, thyme and bay leaf, stirring all the time, and bring to the boil. Simmer on a very low heat for about 1 hour. Just before serving, dissolve the yeast extract in a little of the soup liquid, then return to the saucepan and stir to mix it through. Remove the bay leaf and thyme before serving.

Lentil Soup

vf

This comforting soup is also nice cooked with a few florets of cauliflower.

Sauté the onion and garlic in the oil for about 10 minutes. Add the lentils, carrot and stock. Bring to the boil and simmer gently for about 20 minutes until the lentils are soft and yellow. Liquidise the soup to a smooth texture. Add the lemon juice, parsley, herbs, salt and (plenty of) black pepper. Reheat to serve.

To make Spicy Lentil Soup, add the extra ingredients. Fry the spices with the onion and garlic, adding the soya sauce with the stock.

Ingredients

1 onion, peeled and chopped
2 cloves garlic, peeled and chopped
2 tbsp sunflower oil
225g/8oz split red lentils
1 medium carrot, scrubbed and sliced
1.15 litres/2 pints vegetable stock
1–2 tbsp lemon juice
1 tbsp parsley
1 tbsp mixed herbs
salt and pepper

for *Spicy Lentil Soup*, **add**
2 tsp curry powder
1 tsp ground coriander
1 tbsp soya sauce, or to taste

Ingredients

8 large flat mushrooms
50g/2oz wholemeal breadcrumbs
1 tbsp onion, peeled and very finely
    chopped
1 tbsp yeast extract
1 tbsp hot water
1 tbsp tomato purée
1 tbsp milk or soya milk
15g/½oz margarine, melted

Separate the mushroom caps and stalks, and chop the stalks finely. Put the chopped stalks into a bowl with the breadcrumbs and onion.

Dissolve the yeast extract in the hot water and stir in the tomato purée. Add this to the breadcrumb mixture with the milk or soya milk, and mix well. Put the mushroom caps, smooth side down, onto a lightly greased baking tray. Spoon equal amounts of the stuffing mixture into the mushroom caps, then pour a little of the melted margarine over the top of each mushroom.

Bake near the top of the oven at 200°C/400°F/gas mark 6 for 10 minutes.

Garlic Mushroom Toast ⅴ

Ingredients

Melt the margarine and oil in a saucepan, and add the garlic and mushrooms. Fry for 4–5 minutes, stirring all the time. Meanwhile, toast the bread lightly, cut it in half and put onto a hot plate. Spoon the mushrooms onto the toast and pour the remaining garlic butter on top.

If you are doing this for a starter, you could cut rings out of the toast with a scone-cutter for nicer presentation. Or better still, press the bread into a muffin tin, trimming the edges off the top so it will fit neatly. Brush the inside of the bread with some oil, and bake at about 150°C/300°F/gas mark 2 for 10 minutes. Put the bread case on a plate with some salad, and fill with the mushroom mix.

25g/1oz margarine
2 tbsp olive oil
2–3 cloves garlic, peeled and finely chopped
225g/8oz small mushrooms, wiped and quartered or thickly sliced
4 thick slices wholemeal or granary bread

Mushroom and Avocado Salad

Ingredients

Place the mushrooms in a bowl and stir in the lemon juice and salt. Leave them to marinate for at least 30 minutes. This marinating will 'cook' the mushrooms a little, extracting some of their juices. When you are ready to serve, stir the cream through the mushrooms.

Wash and shred the lettuce and place on four plates. Cut the avocados in half, then peel and chop them. Stir the avocados gently through the mushroom and cream mixture. Place a portion of mushroom and avocado mixture on each plate, and serve with the fresh bread.

450g/1lb small white button mushrooms, wiped and sliced
1 tsp lemon juice
½ tsp salt or to taste
150ml/5fl oz sour or fresh cream
1 iceberg lettuce
2 ripe avocados
fresh crisp bread to serve with the salad

Ingredients

4 medium tomatoes
100–125g/4oz cooked red lentils
¼ onion, peeled and very finely
    chopped
1 tsp dried thyme
½ tbsp tomato paste or purée
pinch of demerara sugar
dash of soya sauce
freshly ground black pepper to taste
25g/1oz vegetarian cheese, grated

To make this vegan, simply leave out the cheese.

Slice the tops off the tomatoes, reserving them, and scoop out the insides. Place the tomato pulp in a bowl together with the rest of the ingredients except the cheese, and mix thoroughly. Fill each tomato skin with a quarter of the mixture, then place a quarter of the cheese on each. Put the tomato lids back on top.

Place the stuffed tomatoes on a greased ovenproof dish and bake at 200°C/400°F/gas mark 6 for approximately 25 minutes.

Mushroom Vol-au-Vents   v

A nice variation on this dish is to use a mixture of button mushrooms and some of the more exotic mushrooms now available, such as shitake or oyster. For a party, you can make multiples of the recipe by preparing both the vol-au-vents and the filling ahead of time, but don't fill the pastry cases until just before you need them or they'll go soggy! Can be eaten hot or cold.

Bake the vol-au-vent cases according to the packet instructions. In the meantime, put the mushrooms in a small saucepan and gently fry them in the margarine for 4–5 minutes, or until soft. Add the pepper and mixed herbs.

Mix the cornflour with a little of the milk to form a paste. Pour just enough milk over the mushrooms to cover them. Bring to the boil, then gradually add the cornflour paste, stirring constantly, until the mixture thickens. If you are serving this hot, add the hot filling to the vol-au-vent cases as soon as they come out of the oven.

Ingredients

12 medium-size frozen vol-au-vent
  cases (non-animal fat brand)
12 medium button mushrooms, wiped
  and finely chopped
40g/1½oz margarine
freshly ground black pepper
½ tsp dried mixed herbs
2 tsp cornflour
milk or soya milk
salt to taste

Ingredients

150g/5oz chick-peas soaked overnight,
   or for at least 8 hours
1 clove garlic, peeled
2 tbsp lemon juice
1 tsp ground coriander
1 tsp ground cumin
1 tsp garam masala
1 tbsp dried parsley
chilli powder to taste
salt and pepper

Falafel   vf

This is a classic snack from the Middle East, usually eaten in pitta pockets with shredded lettuce, sliced cucumber and tomato. Falafel freezes well for about 2 weeks (any longer and the spices go musty), and can be cooked from frozen as long as you don't make them any bigger than walnut-sized.

Thoroughly rinse and drain the chick-peas. Process all the ingredients together very finely. Make small walnut-sized balls, squeezing the balls well to make sure they hold together. Fry in hot oil for 3–4 minutes until they are nicely browned. It's best to shallow-fry them, turning them only once, as bits break off and the oil can't be used again later.

Main Courses

Ingredients

4 medium-sized peppers, red, green
    or preferred colour
100–125g/4oz ground almonds
75g/3oz vegetarian cheddar cheese,
    grated
50g/2oz wholemeal breadcrumbs
2 large tomatoes, finely chopped
100–125g/4oz mushrooms, wiped and
    finely chopped
6 tbsp vegetable stock
1 clove garlic, peeled and chopped
salt and pepper

Peppers Stuffed with Almonds

You will find the food processor very handy for chopping and grating all the ingredients.

Cut the peppers in half vertically, and wash them, removing the seeds first. Put the halves into a saucepan with plenty of cold water and bring to the boil. Take off the heat straightaway, and drain them, then put onto a lightly greased, shallow, ovenproof dish.

Put the nuts, cheese, breadcrumbs, tomatoes, mushrooms, stock and garlic into a bowl and mix together, adding plenty of salt and pepper to taste. Divide the mixture equally between the pepper halves.

Bake uncovered for about 40 minutes at 190°C/375°F/gas mark 5.

Serving Suggestion
Serve with a contrasting coloured vegetable, and new or roast potatoes.

Mushroom and Nut Roast vf

As a variation, try shaping this mixture into burgers, coating with chick-pea flour mix (see p. 31) and breadcrumbs, and frying them. For this, and all roast recipes, you can choose to line along the length of your loaf tin with baking parchment — this makes the roasts turn out much more easily.

Fry the onions in the oil over a low heat for 10 minutes, or until soft, then add the mushrooms and fry for a further 2 minutes. Turn off the heat and add all the remaining ingredients, adding a little more water if the mixture seems a bit dry. It shouldn't be sloppy, but should cling together when it's pressed.

Generously grease a 450g/1lb loaf tin with margarine, then spoon the mixture into the tin. Press it down well, smoothing the top with a spatula or the back of a spoon.

Bake the roast at 180°C/350°F/gas mark 4 for 1 hour. When cooked, loosen the roast with a butter knife around the edges of the tin and turn it out onto a warm serving plate.

Serving Suggestion
New potatoes or roast potatoes, with vegetarian gravy and glazed carrots, go well with this dish.

Ingredients

1 onion, peeled and chopped
2 tbsp olive oil
450g/1lb mushrooms, wiped and
    chopped
50g/2oz ground almonds
50g/2oz ground cashew nuts
225g/8oz wholemeal breadcrumbs
275–300ml/10fl oz vegetable stock
1 tsp yeast extract
1 tsp mixed herbs
salt and pepper to taste

Ingredients

225g/8oz black-eyed beans, soaked and cooked, i.e. 450g/1lb cooked weight
400g/14oz tin chopped tomatoes
275–300ml/10fl oz water or stock (for stock, you can use water in which the beans have been cooked)
1 onion, peeled and chopped
1 clove garlic, peeled and finely chopped
2 tbsp tomato purée
1 small green pepper, chopped (optional)
2 tbsp dried parsley
2 tbsp dried basil
225g/8oz button mushrooms, cleaned and sliced
225g/8oz frozen peas or sweetcorn (or a mixture, for a very colourful dish)

You can use any beans in this simple, but very tasty, casserole.

Put all the ingredients, except the peas and/or sweetcorn, into a large saucepan, bring them to the boil and simmer for 15 minutes. Add the peas and/or sweetcorn. Bring back to the boil and simmer for another 5 minutes.

Serving Suggestion
Serve with baked or mashed potatoes, or rice.

Lentil Savoury

This dish can be prepared ahead of time. To cook, bake at 180°C/350°F/gas mark 4 for about 30 minutes.

Fry the onions in the margarine for about 10 minutes. Add the lentils, water and herbs, bring to the boil, then cover and simmer gently for about 15 minutes. Add the tomatoes, sugar, tomato purée, salt and pepper, and mix well.

Simmer for 15 minutes, then pour the mixture into a greased ovenproof dish. Cover with the cream and cheese, and grill under a high heat until the cheese has melted.

Serving Suggestion
Serve with boiled or mashed potatoes and a green vegetable.

Ingredients

2 onions, peeled and chopped
50g/2oz margarine
175g/6oz red lentils
575–600ml/1pint water
½ tsp dried mixed herbs
½ tsp thyme
400g/14oz tin of tomatoes
1 tsp demerara sugar
1½ tbsp tomato purée
salt and pepper
575–600ml/1pint sour cream
175g/6oz vegetarian cheddar cheese,
    thinly sliced

Ingredients

1 portion of bread dough (see p. 107)
1 portion tomato sauce (see p. 112)
   — cook it slowly until it reduces
   and becomes nice and thick
1 small onion, peeled and sliced
1 small courgette, washed and sliced
1 small green pepper, de-seeded and
   chopped into 15mm/½" pieces
50g/2oz mushrooms, wiped and sliced
¼ tsp dried basil leaves
¼ tsp dried oregano leaves
100–125g/4oz grated vegetarian
   mozzarella cheese (optional)

These pizzas can be made up ahead of time, and then frozen. Simply cook from frozen, adding about 5 minutes to the cooking time. Another option is to make mini-pizzas, approximately 10cm/4" in diameter. These are lovely for parties, and can also be made in advance and frozen — they will need about 15 minutes' cooking time.

Divide the dough into four, and roll out each portion into a circle, thicker or thinner depending on whether you want 'thick-crust' or 'thin and crispy'. Put a thin layer of tomato sauce on each pizza, then top with the remaining ingredients, putting the cheese on top.

Bake at 210–220°C/425°F/gas mark 7 for about 20–30 minutes (depending on thickness) or until the edge of the crust is crisp.

Serving Suggestion
Serve with a garlicky green salad.

Chick-Pea and Apricot Casserole vf

As a variation to this dish, leave out the pasta, and serve with cooked rice or millet, or steamed couscous. Another variation would be to add some frozen spinach to the stock. Apricots are good to use in cooking because of their high iron content.

Fry the onion gently in the olive oil for several minutes. Add the chick-peas, garlic, courgettes, herbs, spices and seasoning, tomatoes and apricots. Stir everything together and cook for 5 minutes. Finally, add the stock and the pasta, and allow to simmer until the apricots and the pasta are tender — approximately 15–20 minutes.

Serving Suggestion
This dish is good with a simple salad.

Ingredients

1 onion, peeled and chopped
100–125ml/4fl oz olive oil
225g/8oz chick-peas, soaked and cooked (giving 450g/1lb cooked weight — keep the stock), or 450g/1lb tin chick-peas, drained
2–3 cloves garlic, peeled and finely chopped
1 large or 2 small courgettes, washed and sliced
1 tsp dried herb of your choice, e.g. basil, oregano, marjoram
1 tbsp chopped parsley or coriander leaves
1 tsp ground coriander
1 tsp ground cumin
salt and pepper to taste
400g/14oz tin tomatoes
225g/8oz dried apricots
575–600ml/1pint stock or water (you can use the chick-pea stock, topping up if necessary)
100–125g/4oz small pasta shapes (e.g. macaroni or broken spaghetti)

Ingredients

4 medium potatoes, scrubbed and
    thinly sliced
1 onion, peeled and thinly sliced
225g/8oz tin Mexican chilli beans
100–125ml/4fl oz milk or soya milk
1 tsp paprika

Mexican Bean Bake vf

A very quick and easy dish, using store-cupboard ingredients.

Lightly grease a 575–600ml/1-pint ovenproof dish. Layer the potato slices, the onion rings and the beans on the base of the dish. Pour the milk over the vegetables, and sprinkle the paprika on top.

Bake, uncovered, in a moderate oven at 190°C/375°F/gas mark 5, for about 25 minutes or until the vegetables are soft.

Serving Suggestion
Serve with some sweetcorn and peas cooked together.

Barley and Vegetable Stew
vf

Barley is a very traditional native Irish grain, which we don't often use. Here is a lovely recipe using this ingredient.

Roast the barley in a dry saucepan until it just starts to brown, being careful not to burn it. Sauté the vegetables briefly in the oil, then add the barley to the vegetables and sauté for a few more minutes. Stir in the yellow split peas and the stock, and season the stew with salt and pepper.

Bring the water to the boil and simmer until the barley is soft (this will take approximately 1½ hours), checking from time to time that the water does not boil dry.

Serving Suggestion
This simple dish is designed to be eaten as it is, but you could also serve a mixed salad for extra nutrition.

Ingredients

100–125g/4oz pot barley
2 onions, peeled and chopped
1 large carrot, scrubbed and chopped
3 sticks celery, washed and sliced
1 leek, washed and sliced
2 tbsp vegetable oil
100–125g/4oz yellow split peas
850ml/1½ pints vegetable stock
salt and pepper to taste

Ingredients

225g/8oz red lentils
1 onion, peeled and chopped
75g/3oz margarine
575–600ml/1 pint vegetable stock
225g/8oz (approx.) potatoes, peeled, cooked and mashed
100–125g/4oz wholemeal breadcrumbs
1 tbsp fresh parsley, washed and chopped
salt and pepper to taste

Lentil Loaf   vf

This mixture can also be used to make rissoles: shape the mixture, dip into chick-pea flour mix (see p. 31), and coat with breadcrumbs. Shallow-fry until brown on both sides. You can freeze it in the tin before baking — just add 10 minutes to the cooking time if you are cooking from frozen. Or you can freeze slices on a tray, then put them in a freezer bag when they are solid. Two minutes in the microwave and you have the basis for a meal — accompany with some salad or vegetables.

Wash and drain the lentils. Fry them together with the onion in 50g/2oz of the margarine, over a gentle heat, for about 5 minutes. Add the stock and bring to the boil, then simmer very gently until the lentils are soft and fairly dry — about 20 minutes.

Add the potato, breadcrumbs, parsley, salt and pepper, and mix well. Spoon this mixture into a greased 450g/1lb loaf tin, pressing down well. Dot the top with the remaining margarine.

Bake at 180°C/350°F/gas mark 4 for about 30 minutes, until browned.

Serving Suggestion
Serve with Tomato Sauce (see p. 112), and steamed broccoli.

58

Vegetable and Kidney Bean Stew vf

If you have beans, a tin of tomatoes, and some vegetables in the house, you always have the basis for a meal — this is a classic example.

Heat the oil in a large saucepan and add the onion, pepper, carrots, courgette and celery. Put a lid on the pan, and cook over a low heat for 10 minutes, stirring occasionally. Add the mushrooms, tomatoes, kidney beans, salt and pepper. Simmer for a few minutes more until the carrot is soft.

Serving Suggestion
Serve with wholemeal bread and a mixed salad.

2 tbsp sunflower or vegetable oil
I small onion, peeled and sliced
I small red pepper, de-seeded and
  chopped
I medium carrot, scrubbed and diced
I courgette, washed and sliced
I stick of celery, washed and sliced
100–125g/4oz mushrooms, wiped and
  thickly sliced
3 tomatoes, peeled and quartered
225g/8oz tin red kidney beans, or
  225g/8oz home-cooked beans*
salt and freshly ground black pepper
  to taste

* See p. 32 for how to cook kidney beans.

Ingredients

½ small onion, peeled and thinly sliced
1 large tomato, thinly sliced
1 clove garlic, peeled and chopped
1 tbsp olive oil
2 thick slices wholewheat bread
1 tsp marjoram or herb of your
    choice (e.g. basil or oregano)
salt and pepper
6 black olives, stoned and halved

Quick Bread Pizza

For one

A very handy suggestion for a quick dinner or snack. If you are vegetarian, you can top the pizzas with some slices of vegetarian cheese before grilling if you prefer.

Gently fry the onion and garlic for about 10 minutes in the oil. Put the bread under the grill and arrange the tomato slices on top, then spread the garlic and onion mixture over them. Sprinkle with the marjoram and season to taste, then dot with the olives and grill for 4–5 minutes.

Serve at once.

Serving Suggestion
Serve with a green salad or coleslaw.

Stir-Fried Vegetables with Tofu   v

Cook this dish in a wok if you have one; otherwise use a deep frying-pan. You can use different vegetables from those suggested.

Cook the rice before beginning this dish, as it will take longer to cook.

Fry the tofu in the oil over a medium heat, turning occasionally until the cubes are browned on all sides. Add all the vegetables except for the bean sprouts and garlic, and cook for about 5 minutes, stirring constantly, lifting and turning the vegetables.

Add the soya sauce and garlic, and cook over a low heat for another 10 minutes. If the mixture becomes dry, add a little water. Add the bean sprouts and continue to cook for a few minutes.

Serve the tofu and vegetables on a bed of rice.

Serving Suggestion
This dish is complete as it is, although a salad is a good accompaniment.

Ingredients

225g/8oz rice, cooked (see p. 34)
225g/8oz firm tofu, cut into cubes
  approximately 25mm/1" thick
2 tbsp olive oil or vegetable oil
1 onion, peeled, sliced and cut into
  half-moons
6 stalks celery, washed and sliced into
  pieces approximately 6mm/¼"
  thick
1 small bunch of scallions, finely
  chopped
1 small red pepper, finely chopped
1 small green pepper, finely chopped
450g/1lb mushrooms, wiped and cut
  into either halves or quarters
  (depending on the size)
6 tbsp soya sauce
1 clove garlic, peeled and finely
  chopped
225g/8oz bean sprouts (approx.)

Ingredients

225g/8oz brown rice
100–125g/4oz chopped or flaked
　　almonds
3 onions, peeled and chopped
1 clove garlic, peeled and chopped
4 tbsp vegetable oil
2 large aubergines, wiped and diced
　　into cubes approximately 25mm/
　　1" thick
225g/8oz mushrooms, wiped and
　　sliced
1 small red pepper, de-seeded and
　　thinly sliced
1 small green pepper, de-seeded and
　　thinly sliced
juice of 1 lemon
4 large tomatoes, finely chopped
salt and pepper

Paella　　　　　　　　　　　　　　vf

This is an excellent dish for leftover rice. Or if you're organised enough, cook extra specially. It isn't genuine Spanish paella, as the rice and vegetables are cooked separately — apologies to Spaniards!

Cook the rice following the instructions on p. 34.

Meanwhile, toast the almonds under the grill, watching them carefully as they can burn quickly. Gently fry the onions and garlic in the oil for about 10 minutes, then add the aubergines, mushrooms and peppers to the onions. Continue to sauté for a few minutes, then add the rice, lemon juice and seasoning. Stir, and add the tomatoes and almonds, mixing well.

Put on a low heat until the paella is thoroughly heated before serving.

Serving Suggestion
Serve with a large mixed salad.

Stuffed Pancakes

For variety, try other vegetables instead of the mushrooms, such as steamed, chopped broccoli and cauliflower, or diced courgettes.

Put the flour, salt, water and egg into a blender and process until smooth (or blend manually using an egg whisk).

Wipe and slice the mushrooms and sauté in the margarine until tender. Add the flour, stirring, then add the cream and seasoning. Keep the mixture warm.

Fry thin pancakes on one side only in a very small amount of the vegetable oil, then pile them on a plate and keep them warm. Spread the cooked side of the pancakes with the filling, and roll them up.

Finally, fry 2–3 pancakes together in a pan in a small amount of oil, turning them carefully to brown all sides.

Serving Suggestion
Brown rice and a mixed salad go well with this dish.

For the pancakes
100–125g/4oz wholemeal flour
½ tsp salt
275–300ml/10fl oz water
1 free-range egg

For the filling
225g/8oz mushrooms
25g/1oz margarine
½ tsp wholemeal flour
2 tbsp cream
salt, pepper and nutmeg to taste

vegetable oil for frying

Ingredients

450g/1lb potatoes, peeled and sliced
2 medium parsnips, scrubbed (or
    peeled if they're not the best), and
    sliced
2 medium leeks, finely chopped
    (greens as well as whites)
225ml/8fl oz soya milk
450g/1lb kale or cabbage, finely
    chopped
1 large clove garlic, peeled and
    chopped
½ tsp grated nutmeg
salt and pepper to taste
2 tbsp margarine

Colcannon

This is one of the very few traditional Irish dishes which are vegetarian.

Cook the potatoes and parsnips in sufficient water until they are tender. While these are cooking, simmer the leeks in the milk until soft.

Cook the kale or cabbage in water until soft, then drain well. Also drain the potatoes, then season with the garlic, nutmeg, salt and pepper, and mash them well. Add the cooked leeks and milk (being careful not to break down the leeks too much).

Blend in the kale or cabbage and the margarine — the texture should be like smooth, buttery potato with well-distributed pieces of leek and kale.

Serving Suggestion
Garnish with parsley before serving.
This dish can also be served with steamed sliced carrots and a vegetarian burger.

Baked Savoury Roll　　　　　　　　vf

If you use bought pastry for this dish, make sure there are no animal fats in the ingredients. All the vegetables need to be chopped — this can be done in the food processor. Process the onion first, then while it's cooking add the rest of the vegetables and process them. A nice variation on this dish is to make individual pasties.

Heat the oil and cook the onions for 2–3 minutes. Add the remaining vegetables and cook for about 3–4 minutes more, then take off the heat and add the nuts, herbs, yeast extract and cornflour. Mix well and leave to cool.

Roll the pastry into a large square approximately 3mm/$\frac{1}{8}$" thick, then spread the vegetable mixture evenly to 15mm/½" from the edge. Dampen the edges and roll up firmly like a Swiss roll, then press down the edges.

Bake in a hot oven at 200°C/400°F/gas mark 6 for 30 minutes.

Serving Suggestion
Serve with Red Pepper Sauce (see p. 111) and a mixed salad.

Ingredients

2 tbsp vegetable oil
1 onion, peeled and finely chopped
¼ small cabbage, finely chopped
2 medium carrots, scrubbed and finely chopped
1 leek, washed and finely chopped
100–125g/4oz mushrooms, finely chopped
25g/1oz chopped nuts of your choice
1 tsp mixed herbs
1 tsp yeast extract
1 tsp cornflour
225g/8oz shortcrust pastry

Ingredients

275g/10oz tin condensed mushroom
   soup
275–300ml/10fl oz milk or water
1 tsp vegetable stock granules or
   1 vegetable stock cube
1 tsp Marmite
900g/2lb potatoes, scrubbed and cut
   into thin slices
freshly ground black pepper to taste
2 onions, peeled and sliced into rings
100–125g/4oz mushrooms, wiped and
   sliced
100–125g/4oz vegetarian cheddar
   cheese, grated

Potato and Mushroom Bake f

Check the mushroom soup to make sure it's vegetarian — no chicken or meat bouillon. To speed up this dish, the potato slices can be partly cooked in advance, either in the microwave or in a pan of water. If you do this, use the cooking liquid instead of milk or water.

Mix the soup and milk or water together, and heat in the microwave or in a saucepan. Stir in the vegetable stock and Marmite until they have blended into the soup.

Arrange a layer of potato slices in the bottom of a large casserole dish, and sprinkle them with pepper. Put a layer of onion rings, then a layer of mushrooms, on top of the potatoes, then pour some of the soup mixture over the top. Sprinkle with some of the cheese. Keep adding layers of potatoes, pepper, onions, mushrooms, soup and cheese, until all the ingredients are used up, ending with a good sprinkling of cheese.

Bake at 210–220°C/425°F/gas mark 7 for 50–60 minutes, or 30–40 minutes if the potatoes are pre-cooked.

Serving Suggestion
This dish is particularly tasty served with steamed broccoli.

Spanish Omelette

This classic, quick dish serves one — just multiply by the number of portions you require.

Heat the oil in a frying-pan. Add the green pepper, onion and mushrooms and cook slowly until soft. When these are ready, add the potato cubes and chopped tomato to the frying-pan and heat through.

Break the eggs into a bowl, add the water, salt and pepper, and beat lightly with a fork, just enough to break up the eggs.

When the vegetable mix is hot, pour the egg over it and cook until the underside is firm but the top still runny. Place the pan under a hot grill for 30 seconds or until the top has just set. Loosen the sides and base of the omelette and slide it out onto a warm plate to serve.

Serving Suggestion
Serve with some brown sauce and garden peas, or a crispy salad.

1 tbsp margarine or olive oil
1 small green pepper, finely chopped
100–125g/4oz onion, peeled and
    chopped
50g/2oz mushrooms, sliced
175g/6oz cooked potato, cubed
75g/3oz tomatoes, chopped
2 large free-range eggs
3 tsp water
salt and freshly ground black pepper

Ingredients

For a 21cm/8" round pie:

Make pastry following the recipe for
  Brown Shortcrust Pastry (p. 108).

2 onions, peeled and chopped
sunflower oil for frying
275–300ml/10fl oz of vegetable stock
1 tbsp tomato purée
1 tbsp medium-strength soya sauce
salt and pepper to taste
50g/2oz wholemeal flour
175g/6oz small white, tight button
  mushrooms
50g/2oz garden peas
soya milk for glaze

Stephen's Savoury Mushroom Pie   vf

This is a recipe from Ita West which, as she says, is 'so "meaty" that carnivores wouldn't know that it was vegan'.

Fry the onions in the oil in a saucepan until they start to turn brown. Add 175ml/6fl oz of the stock, and bring to the boil. Boil until the onions are completely soft and cooked (approximately 10 minutes), then add the tomato purée, soya sauce and seasoning.

Mix the remaining 100–125ml/4fl oz of stock with the flour into a thin paste. Add this to the saucepan, stirring well. Simmer until a thick sauce has formed, then set aside.

Slice the mushrooms thickly, and add these with the peas to the sauce. Bring back to the boil, then set aside.

Grease the pie dish with margarine, or line with greaseproof paper. Roll out half the pastry and press it into the dish. Pour the sauce into this and cover it with the rest of the pastry. Brush the top of the pie with soya milk, and decorate the pie top as required. Bake at 200°C/400°F/gas mark 6 for 25 minutes.

Serving suggestion
Roast potatoes and baby carrots go well with this pie.

Pasta Recipes

Pasta is understandably a mainstay of vegetarian cookery — it's quick, healthy and cheap.
You can also experiment with some of the bought pasta sauces, both for pouring and baking — as usual check
the ingredients for slaughterhouse by-products. Be careful, though — a lot of these sauces are very high in fat,
so use sparingly, and balance the meal with lots of low-fat food.

Ingredients

1 onion, peeled and finely chopped
1–2 cloves garlic, peeled and finely
    chopped
2 tbsp olive oil
225g/8oz brown lentils, cooked as per
    instructions on p. 32 (reserve the
    liquid)
400g/14oz tin chopped tomatoes
1 carrot, scrubbed and sliced
1 red or green pepper, de-seeded and
    sliced
1 stick celery, washed and sliced
575–600ml/1 pint vegetable stock (use
    the stock from the lentils, topping
    up as necessary, or use 575–
    600ml/1 pint water and a stock
    cube)
100–125ml/4fl oz red wine (optional)
1 tsp yeast extract
2 tbsp fresh basil, or oregano
2 tbsp fresh parsley
salt and pepper to taste
325–350g/12oz spaghetti

Spaghetti Bolognese vf

This is a simple, but very handy recipe, which has lots of variations. Use the Bolognese mixture, topped with mashed potato, to make shepherd's pie. Add a tin of drained kidney beans, and replace the herbs and wine with chilli powder, for a nice chilli non carne. Instead of using the brown lentils, you can use TVP mince — soak it in 575–600ml/1 pint of boiled water for about 10 minutes, and simply use (this water will count as your stock). You can vary the vegetables according to what you have, and your own preferences. You can batch-cook the Bolognese sauce and freeze, so you have handy the makings of many dishes.

Gently fry the onion and garlic in the oil for about 10 minutes, until soft. Add all the other ingredients, then bring to the boil, and simmer for about 20 minutes, until the vegetables are cooked and the liquid is reduced to a nice consistency.

Meanwhile, cook the spaghetti in plenty of boiling water, following the instructions on the packet.

Serving Suggestion
Serve with a mixed green salad.

Ingredients

This easy and simple dish can also be cooked with bought pesto. Check the ingredients to make sure it's vegetarian — at least one brand has chicken bouillon in it.

Cook the spaghetti in a large amount of water according to the instructions on the packet.

To make the pesto, remove the stalks from the basil and put the leaves into a blender with the garlic, pine kernels and olive oil. Blend the mixture at a medium speed until it becomes a thick purée.

Drain the spaghetti and add the pesto on top. Sprinkle with the Parmesan cheese (if using).

325–350g/12oz wholewheat spaghetti
50g/2oz fresh basil
2 cloves garlic, peeled
40g/1½oz pine kernels
4fl oz olive oil
25g/1oz grated vegetarian Parmesan cheese (optional)
salt to taste

Serving Suggestion
Serve with a green salad and some crusty bread.

Ingredients

325–350g/12oz dried pasta e.g. spirals
   or tagliatelle
100–125g/4oz walnut pieces
2 cloves garlic, peeled and chopped
2 tbsp olive oil
100–125g/4oz tofu
2 tbsp fresh basil
1 tbsp fresh parsley
salt and pepper to taste
1 tbsp soya sauce
1 tsp yeast extract

Be careful when adding salt to this dish, as both soya sauce and yeast extract are quite salty already.

Cook the pasta according to the instructions on the packet, then drain. While it's cooking, process all the other ingredients in a blender or food processor, adding water as necessary to make a smooth sauce. Mix the sauce with the hot pasta and serve immediately.

Serving Suggestion
Serve with a garlicky green salad.

Spinach and Tofu Lasagne

This unusual dish is very tasty, and the tofu makes it high in protein.

Cook the spinach in a small amount of water. Drain, and set aside the liquid.

Meanwhile, cook the lasagne according to the instructions on the packet, adding the oil to the boiling water (this isn't necessary if you use 'no-cook' lasagne). When it's ready, drain off most of the hot water and add cold water to the pan so that the pasta will be cool enough to handle.

To make the filling, blend the tofu, spinach, herbs, onion, salt, pepper and garlic, adding a little of the spinach cooking water, if needed, to make the blending easier.

Lightly oil a lasagne dish, then layer the ingredients in the following order — lasagne, filling, cheese sauce — until all the ingredients are used up. Finish with a layer of the sauce.

Bake at 180°C/350°F/gas mark 4 for 30 minutes.

Serving Suggestion
Green salad and garlic bread are delicious with lasagne.

Ingredients

450g/1lb frozen chopped spinach
225g/8oz plain or wholewheat lasagne
1 tbsp vegetable oil
225g/8oz firm tofu
2 tbsp basil or mixed herbs
1 onion, peeled and chopped
salt and freshly ground black pepper
1 clove garlic, peeled and finely
    chopped
1 portion Cheese Sauce (see p. 110)

Ingredients

250g/9oz macaroni or other pasta
    shapes
50g/2oz margarine
1 onion, peeled and chopped
100–125g/4oz button mushrooms,
    wiped and sliced
2 cloves garlic, peeled and chopped
2 tsp vegetable stock granules or
    2 vegetable stock cubes
½ tsp Marmite
plenty of freshly ground black pepper
100–125g/4oz vegetarian cheddar
    cheese, grated
2 tsp cornflour
275–300ml/10fl oz milk or soya milk

Here's our recipe for this classic dish. A nice variation would be to cook some broccoli and cauliflower florets with the pasta.

Cook the pasta until just soft (approximately 5–10 minutes), taking care not to overcook. Drain the pasta and add half the margarine, stirring in to keep the pasta from sticking together.

Melt the remaining margarine in a saucepan and gently fry the onions until soft (approximately 10 minutes). Add the mushrooms and garlic and cook for a few minutes more. When these are ready, add the stock granules, Marmite and pepper, and stir until they are blended in.

Mix the cornflour with a little of the milk to form a thin paste. Add the rest of the milk to the pasta and stir in with the onion mixture and the cheese. Put the pan back onto a low heat, stirring occasionally until the mixture begins to bubble.

Add the cornflour paste gradually, and keep stirring until the sauce thickens, using more or less cornflour paste as necessary.

Serving Suggestion
Serve with a green salad or a green vegetable, and some slices of crusty bread.

Curries

Curry dishes are usually very popular with vegetarians and non-vegetarians alike, and can be made with almost any vegetable. You can vary the dish by serving it with brown rice or naan bread, and you can of course make it as hot and spicy, or as mild, as you like.

Ingredients

1 large potato, scrubbed and cut into chunks
50g/2oz brown lentils
50g/2oz green lentils
50g/2oz unflavoured TVP chunks
100–125g/4oz mushrooms, wiped and quartered
200g/7oz tin baked beans
150g/5oz (or ½ jar) mild curry sauce
1–2 tsp hot curry powder
2 tbsp tomato sauce or purée
salt to taste
1 tsp sugar
50ml/2fl oz vegetable or olive oil

Adjust the amount of curry powder to taste — this recipe is quite mild. This will freeze for about two weeks (any longer and the spices go musty). If reheating, add a little liquid and some more curry paste.

Cook the potato, lentils, TVP chunks and mushrooms in enough water to cover, until the potato is tender (approximately 20 minutes). Drain the excess liquid and keep to one side. Add the baked beans, curry sauce and powder, tomato sauce, salt and sugar. Mix together and simmer gently for a further 5 minutes. Add the vegetable oil, and if the mixture seems too dry, add some of the drained liquid and stir in.

Serving Suggestion
This curry goes well with either naan bread or brown rice.

Vegetable Curry vf

This dish is very nutritious in terms of the high vegetable content. You can add some cooked chick-peas as a variation and to add protein. Also, vary the vegetables to suit what you have available. It will freeze for up to two weeks.

Heat 50ml/2fl oz of the water in a saucepan and stir in the spices and curry powder, then simmer until the mixture is reduced by half. Add to the saucepan the rest of the water, the tinned tomatoes, the potatoes, onion, carrot and cauliflower. Bring to the boil and simmer, covered, for approximately 10 minutes, or until the potato is just soft.

Finally, add the peas, broccoli and courgette, and simmer, covered, for a further 5 minutes, or until the liquid is reduced slightly and the vegetables are soft.

Serving Suggestion
Ladle into the centre of a ring of brown rice.

Ingredients

575–600ml/1 pint water
1 tsp ground cumin
1 tsp ground coriander
1 tsp garam masala
1 tsp curry powder
400g/14oz tin chopped tomatoes
2 medium potatoes, scrubbed and cut
   into cubes approximately 25mm/
   1" thick
1 onion, peeled and sliced
1 large carrot, scrubbed and sliced
450g/1lb cauliflower, washed and
   separated into small florets
100–125g/4oz frozen peas
325–350g/12oz broccoli, washed and
   separated into small florets
2 courgettes, washed and chopped
   into pieces approximately
   25mm/1" in size

Ingredients

3 tbsp sunflower oil

2 whole red chillies (optional)

2 tsp mustard seeds

1 cauliflower, washed and separated
   into small florets

4 large potatoes, well scrubbed and
   cut into cubes approximately
   25mm/1" thick

2 green chillies, de-seeded and very
   finely chopped*

400g/14oz tin chopped tomatoes

½ tsp turmeric

½ tsp chilli powder or cayenne
   pepper (or to taste)

1 tsp cumin powder

1 tsp coriander powder

salt to taste

*   Always wash your hands after
    handling chillies, and avoid contact
    between your chilli-ed hands and
    your eyes.

Cauliflower and Potato Curry   vf

Heat the oil in a wok or deep frying-pan, and add the red chillies, mustard seeds, cauliflower and potatoes. Add the green chillies, together with the tomatoes, turmeric, chilli powder, cumin, coriander and salt.

Put a lid on the pan and cook over a medium heat for approximately 15–20 minutes. Stir the curry occasionally, adding a little water if it sticks. Be sure to remove the red chillies before serving!

Serving Suggestion
Serve with brown rice or naan bread.

Burgers

Remember, if it can be mashed it can be burgerised! Try combinations of your choice of potato, cooked vegetables (root vegetables are particularly good), mashed beans, grated cheese, millet or rice.

All burgers can be shaped and frozen, but make sure you defrost them before cooking.

Unlike meat burgers, which need a long cooking time, these really only need reheating and crisping.

Burgers are usually dipped in beaten egg before being coated with breadcrumbs. We have specified chick-pea flour mix. This is 2 tbsp chick-pea flour, mixed with a fork with 4 tbsp water — if you find you need extra, just mix up some more.

Ingredients

1 onion, peeled and chopped
1 clove garlic, peeled and finely
    chopped
2 tbsp olive oil
175g/6oz chick-peas, soaked and
    cooked, giving 325–350g/
    12oz cooked weight
450g/1lb potatoes, cooked and
    mashed, not too wet
2 tsp curry powder
1 tsp chilli powder
1 tbsp dried or fresh parsley
salt and pepper
chick-pea flour mix (see p. 79)
breadcrumbs to coat the burgers
vegetable oil for frying

Chick-Pea and Potato Croquettes   vf

These burgers are easy, if a little time-consuming to make, but well worth the effort. Don't forget you can make double the quantity and freeze half, giving you two meals for the effort of one.

Sauté the onion and garlic in the oil for about 10 minutes, until soft. While they are cooking, mash the cooked chick-peas roughly, then mix them with the mashed potato — not too thoroughly, to retain texture. Add the onion and garlic. Add the curry powder, chilli powder and parsley, then season with salt and pepper.

Form the mixture into croquettes and dip them into the chick-pea flour mix, and then into the breadcrumbs. Fry in hot oil, or alternatively bake for 30–40 minutes at 200°C/400°F/gas mark 6, turning them over halfway to brown both sides evenly.

Serving Suggestion
These are lovely with Tomato Sauce (see p. 112) and a green vegetable, or alternatively with Mint and Yoghurt Sauce (see p. 110) and a salad.

Millet Rissoles vf

As a (vegan) variation, use 100–125g/4oz of cooked red lentils instead of the cheese.

Gently fry the onion and garlic in the oil for about 10 minutes. Put the millet into the saucepan and stir for a minute to brown slightly. Add the water and a little salt, and bring to the boil. Turn down to a very low simmer, cover and cook for approximately 25 minutes, or until all the water is absorbed, checking occasionally to make sure that the mixture does not dry out and start to burn.

Add the cheese, mixed herbs, paprika, basil and parsley, and a small amount of pepper, and mix well. Leave for a few minutes until the mixture is cool enough to handle (but don't leave it too long, as it will set hard), then shape into approximately eight rissoles. Dip the rissoles into the chick-pea mix, then cover them in breadcrumbs.

Shallow-fry or put under a hot grill until golden brown, turning once.

Serving Suggestion
Serve hot with gravy or Tomato Sauce (see p. 112) and a green vegetable.

Ingredients

1 onion, peeled and finely chopped
2 cloves garlic, peeled and finely chopped
2 tbsp olive or vegetable oil
150g/5oz millet
425ml/15fl oz water
100–125g/4oz vegetarian cheddar cheese, grated
1 tsp mixed herbs
pinch paprika
1 tsp basil
1 tbsp fresh parsley
salt and pepper to taste
chick-pea flour mix (see p. 79)
wholemeal breadcrumbs to coat rissoles

Ingredients

2 small onions, peeled and finely chopped
2 tbsp olive oil
450g/1lb potatoes, peeled and cooked
450g/1lb packet frozen spinach, thawed and thoroughly drained
50g/2oz ground cashew nuts
50g/2oz ground sunflower seeds
2 tbsp fresh parsley
sunflower or vegetable oil

Spinach Burgers   vf

Thaw the spinach first, and cook the potato if you don't have any already cooked.

Fry the onions in a little oil on a low heat in a large pan. Mash the potatoes and add them to the pan with the spinach, then sauté for 10 minutes, stirring. Add the nuts, seeds and parsley, and stir well.

Leave the mixture to cool, then with floured hands form into burgers. Shallow-fry until brown on both sides, or grill until brown, turning once.

Serving Suggestion
Serve with Mint and Yoghurt Sauce (see p. 110) and a variety of salads.

Soya Recipes

Here are a few recipes using packet soya-based meat equivalents. These are more processed than a lot of vegetarian ingredients, but are certainly healthier than their meat equivalents. Most long-term vegetarians use these only occasionally, but they are great for people getting used to a vegetarian diet, as they can be used in familiar recipes, and are also good for a lone vegetarian in a family.

Ingredients

1 packet vegetarian soya sausage mix
1 apple, cored and diced
50g/2oz wholemeal breadcrumbs
1 small onion, peeled and finely
    chopped

Apple and pork are a classic combination — here's our vegetarian version.

Make up the sausage mix as instructed on the packet, then divide the mixture into three and roll out into three rectangles, each to fit the base of a 900g/2lb loaf tin.

Combine the apples, breadcrumbs and onion, and divide into two. Put one rectangle of sausage mix into the greased loaf tin, and put half the apple mixture on top. Put another sausage-mix rectangle on top of that, then the rest of the apple mixture, and finally the last rectangle.

Place on a baking sheet, and bake in a moderate oven at 180°C/350°F/gas mark 4 for 30–40 minutes.

Alternatively:
Make up the sausage mix as instructed, then roll the mix into a large rectangle on greaseproof paper. Spread the apple mixture on top, and roll up like a Swiss roll.

Place on a baking sheet, and bake in a moderate oven at 180°C/350°F/gas mark 4 for 30–40 minutes.

Serving Suggestion
This roast goes well with potato salad, coleslaw and a green salad.

Cider is a classic with pork dishes, so we're taking advantage of that in this vegetarian version.

Make up the sausage mix according to the instructions on the packet, then roll into sausage shapes. Sauté the sausages in the oil and add the breadcrumbs. Turn up the heat and cook until brown.

Add the wine or cider, tomatoes, onion and celery, then bring to the boil and simmer for 10 minutes. Add the salt, pepper and herbs, and simmer for 10 minutes more. Remove the bay leaf before serving.

Serving Suggestion
This is lovely with mashed potato and garden peas.

Ingredients

1 packet vegetarian soya sausage mix
2 tbsp vegetable oil
2 tbsp wholemeal breadcrumbs
425ml/15fl oz vegan wine or cider as preferred
2 tomatoes, sliced
1 onion, peeled and sliced
1 stalk celery, washed and chopped
salt and pepper to taste
½ tsp thyme
1 bay leaf

Ingredients

½ packet vegetarian soya burger mix
1 large potato, peeled, cooked and
    mashed
2 tbsp onion, peeled and finely
    chopped
pepper to taste
½ tsp salt
½ tsp mixed herbs
vegetable oil to fry

Soya Burgers vf

You can simply make up the burgers according to the instructions, but this recipe provides more carbohydrate and is a little bit different.

Make up the burger mix according to the packet instructions.

Add the potato, onion and seasonings, then shape into burgers. Fry the burgers gently in oil, turning once, until brown on both sides.

Serving Suggestion
Serve in a burger bap with all the trimmings.

86

Recipes for Special Occasions

These recipes are a little more complicated than most of the other recipes,
but would be lovely for Sunday dinner, Christmas, or another special occasion.

Ingredients

2 large onions, peeled and chopped
50g/2oz butter
2 tsp mixed herbs
175g/6oz pine nuts, finely ground
175g/6oz cashew nuts, ground
175g/6oz fresh wholemeal
　breadcrumbs
3 tbsp lemon juice
salt and freshly ground black pepper
　to taste
225g/8oz cooked fresh or tinned
　chestnuts, mashed

Pine and Cashew Nut Roast with Chestnut Stuffing vf

Gently sauté the onions in the butter with the herbs for about 10 minutes. Take off the heat. Place one-third of the fried onion in a bowl and put to one side. Add the nuts, two-thirds of the breadcrumbs, and most of the lemon juice and seasoning to the fried onion in the saucepan. Stir together well, adding a little water if the mixture seems too dry — it should be quite dry, but it should hold together if pressed.

To make the stuffing, add the rest of the breadcrumbs and the mashed chestnut to the onion in the bowl, mix them together well, and season with salt, pepper and a little lemon juice.

Line along the length of a 900g/2lb loaf tin with well-greased baking parchment, then spoon half the nut mixture into the tin, pressing down well. Spread the chestnut mixture on top, level it, then spoon the rest of the nut mixture on top, pressing down well.

Cover with a piece of baking foil and bake for 1 hour at 190°C/375°F/ gas mark 5. Remove the foil, and continue to bake for another 15 minutes until lightly browned. Carefully remove the roast, first sliding a blunt knife down the sides of the loaf tin to loosen the edges.

Serving Suggestion
Garnish with sprigs of parsley, and serve with boiled new potatoes with butter, broccoli and a light vegetarian gravy.

Courgette Pie

Ingredients

This Greek-style pie uses filo pastry, which can be found in the freezer section of the supermarket (check the packet to make sure vegetable fat is used).

Roast the pine nuts for approximately 5 minutes at 180°C/350°F/gas mark 4.

Meanwhile, finely chop the courgettes, onion, garlic, basil and parsley. Fry the onion in the olive oil until it begins to soften (about 5 minutes). Add the courgettes and cook for 4 minutes. Stir in the garlic, herbs and wine and cook for another 4 minutes, then remove from the heat. Stir in the eggs and cheese.

Brush a lasagne dish with a little of the butter or oil, then put a sheet of the filo pastry on the bottom of the dish. Brush again with the butter or oil and repeat the process, sprinkling some pine kernels between the layers, until half the pastry is used. Spread the filling on top of the pastry, then continue to layer up the remaining sheets.

Bake at 200°C/400°F/gas mark 6 for 40–50 minutes or until well browned.

Serving Suggestion
Serve with a fresh green salad and garlic bread.

75g/3oz pine nuts
225g/8oz courgettes
1 small onion, peeled
1 large clove garlic
2 tbsp fresh basil
3 tbsp parsley
2 tbsp olive oil
50ml/2fl oz white wine
2 free-range eggs, beaten
50g/2oz vegetarian Parmesan, grated
75g/3oz vegetarian feta cheese, finely chopped
8 tbsp melted butter or olive oil
135g/4–5oz (or ½ packet) filo pastry

Ingredients

Red Pepper Sauce (see p. 111)
450g/1lb fresh or frozen spinach
    (defrosted)
4 free-range eggs, separated
150ml/5fl oz sour or fresh cream
salt and pepper to taste
pinch of grated nutmeg
100–125g/4oz vegetarian cream
    cheese
¼ tsp mixed herbs

Spinach Roulade with Red Pepper Sauce

Try to have the eggs at room temperature, so the whites will beat more easily.

Cook the spinach in a little water (if using fresh) until tender, then drain thoroughly and chop finely. Place in a medium-sized bowl with the egg yolks and the cream. Add the salt, pepper and nutmeg, and mix well.

Whisk the egg whites until they are stiff but not dry, then fold them into the spinach mixture. Put the mixture carefully into a 18x23cm/ 7"x9" Swiss roll tin lined with greaseproof paper.

Bake for 15 minutes at 190°C/375°F/gas mark 5 until it is firm and golden. When it's cool enough to handle, turn out the roll onto greaseproof paper and remove the backing paper.

While the spinach mixture is baking, blend together the cream cheese and herbs. Having removed the spinach bake from the oven, spread the cheese and herb filling on top, leaving the edges free. Ease the spinach bake gently into a roll, and put onto a plate with the join downwards.

Put the roll into the oven for a few minutes at 150°C/350°F/gas mark 2, then serve with the Red Pepper Sauce.

Serving Suggestion
A nice salad and some sweetcorn make lovely accompaniments to this dish.

Festive Croustade   v

A croustade is a kind of upside-down dish, with the crusty 'topping' underneath and the vegetables on top. The dish can be made ahead of time, keeping the croustade and topping separate until it's time to cook. When you are ready to cook it, put the topping on the croustade, and heat on a low oven setting for about 20 minutes.

To make the croustade:
Mix together the breadcrumbs, ground almonds and margarine. Add the Brazil nuts, walnuts, garlic, herbs and salt, and mix well. Press the mixture firmly into a well-greased 23cm/9" flan dish.

Bake in a hot oven at 230°C/450°F/gas mark 8, for 10–15 minutes, or until golden brown and crisp — do not allow to burn.

To make the topping:
Sauté the mushrooms in the margarine for about 5 minutes, then stir in the flour and cook for 1–2 minutes. Remove from the heat and gradually add the milk, stirring constantly. Simmer for 10 minutes, stirring, until the mixture is quite thick, then add the nutmeg, salt and pepper.

Spread the topping over the croustade. Slice the tomatoes, and use them to decorate the croustade. Return to a low shelf in the hot oven to heat through, again not allowing the croustade to burn.

Serving Suggestion
Serve with baby new potatoes with butter, and steamed broccoli.

Ingredients

For the croustade
100–125g/4oz wholemeal breadcrumbs
100–125g/4oz ground almonds
50g/2oz margarine
50g/2oz Brazil nut pieces
50g/2oz walnut pieces
1 clove garlic, peeled and finely chopped
1 tsp mixed herbs
a pinch of salt

For the topping
450g/1lb mushrooms, wiped and sliced
50g/2oz margarine
3 tbsp plain flour
425ml/15fl oz milk or soya milk
¼ tsp grated nutmeg
salt and pepper to taste
3 tomatoes

Ingredients

For the filling
2 tbsp olive oil
2 onions, peeled and finely chopped
325–350g/12oz mushrooms, wiped and finely chopped
1 medium leek, washed and finely chopped
225g/8oz ground mixed nuts
100–125g/4oz wholemeal breadcrumbs
1 tbsp soya sauce
salt and pepper to taste
thyme, parsley, and rosemary to taste (or other herbs of your choice)
small quantity of vegetable stock or water if necessary

For the pastry
325–350g/12oz flour
pinch of salt
1 tsp baking powder
100–125g/4oz margarine
100–125ml/4fl oz water
extra boiling water as necessary

Heat the oil in a large saucepan and gently fry the onions for 10 minutes until soft. Add the mushrooms and leek, and cook over a very low heat for 5 minutes until the mushroom juices start to run. Remove from the heat and add all the other filling ingredients to form a thick, but not dry consistency. Add a little stock or water if necessary. Allow to cool.

To make the pastry, sift the flour, salt and baking powder into a large bowl. Cut the margarine into small pieces and melt in a saucepan. Add the cold water and bring to a fierce boil. Immediately pour this liquid into the centre of the flour and mix vigorously with a wooden spoon until glossy. When the mixture is cool enough to handle, knead into a ball.

Divide the mixture and place one-third in an oiled plastic bag to prevent it from drying out. Use the remaining two-thirds to line the base and sides of a 18cm/7" spring-mould, pressing down and moulding into position. Spoon in the filling, pressing down firmly and making a 'dome' shape.

Roll out the remaining pastry to just larger than the tin, and place on top of the pie, pinching the edges together to seal. Trim off any excess pastry, and make decorative leaves for the top of the pie with the trimmings. Cut vents in the lid to allow the steam to escape.

Bake at 210–220°C/425°F/gas mark 7 for 20 minutes. Reduce the heat to 190°C/375°F/gas mark 5 and bake for a further hour. Leave to stand for about 10 minutes, then un-mould and serve with roast potatoes and Spicy Red Cabbage (see p. 99).

Aubergine and Couscous en Croûte

Put the couscous into a large mixing bowl with the sultanas and apricots, and pour the vegetable stock over the top. Mix together well, then leave to soak.

Brush the aubergine slices on both sides with some of the olive oil, and put them under a preheated grill for approximately 5 minutes on each side, or until they are soft and brown. Grill the pepper until the skin is charred, and carefully wrap the pepper in baking foil and leave it to cool. Once cool, remove the skin and cut the flesh into small pieces.

Pour the remaining olive oil into a saucepan and sauté the onion and garlic for 5 minutes until soft. Add the spices and continue to cook, stirring, for another minute.

Using a fork, stir the couscous, loosening it, then add the pepper, tomatoes, onion mixture, almonds, parsley, mint and seasoning, and mix well.

Put the pastry onto a floured surface and roll it into a square approximately 30x30cm/12"x12". Cut the square in half, keeping back some of the trimmings to use as decoration on top. Place one rectangle on a greased baking sheet, and spread half the cranberry sauce over it, leaving a 2.5cm/1" border all around. Spoon half the couscous mixture over the cranberry sauce, still leaving the border, and smooth the top with a spatula.

Ingredients

100–125g/4oz couscous
50g/2oz sultanas
25g/1oz dried apricots, chopped
575–600ml/1 pint hot vegetable stock
1 large aubergine, sliced lengthways
4 tbsp olive oil
1 red pepper, de-seeded and quartered
1 onion, peeled and chopped
2 cloves garlic, minced
1 tbsp ground cinnamon
1 tbsp ground coriander
3 large tomatoes, diced
75g/3oz toasted flaked almonds
2 tbsp fresh parsley, chopped, or 1 tbsp dried
2 tbsp fresh mint, chopped, or 1 tbsp dried
salt and pepper to taste
375g/13oz pack puff pastry (vegetarian)
4 tbsp cranberry sauce
100–125g/4oz vegetarian feta cheese, or vegetarian mozzarella cheese, grated
1 free-range egg, beaten

(continued overleaf)

Put half the aubergine slices on top of the couscous, and sprinkle half the grated cheese over it. Repeat the layers with the remaining couscous mixture, the rest of the aubergine and cheese, and finish with the remaining cranberry sauce.

Brush the pastry border with a little of the beaten egg. If necessary, roll the second rectangle of pastry until it is slightly larger than the first, then carefully place it on top of the layers, and down the sides. Pull the bottom layer up a little until you can press the two sheets of pastry together, then crimp the edges firmly with your thumbs. Glaze the top of the pastry with the remaining beaten egg. With the back of a knife, cut diagonal lines across the pastry — take care not to cut right through! Finally, cut out fancy shapes from the pastry trimmings and use them for decoration.

Bake in the top half of a preheated oven at 210–220°C/425°F/gas mark 7 for approximately 20 minutes, or until golden brown. Take out and leave to cool for 5 minutes before slicing and serving.

Serving Suggestion

This makes a wonderful Christmas dinner centrepiece. It's great served with all the traditional trimmings, or for a lighter alternative, it goes well with a crisp winter salad, served with a creamy yoghurt and lime dressing.

Accompaniments

Ingredients

50g/2oz butter or margarine
50g/2oz sugar
700g/1½lb carrots, scrubbed and
   thinly sliced
3–4 tbsp thick-peel marmalade
150ml/5fl oz water
salt and pepper

Ingredients

450g/1lb Brussels sprouts
handful roasted pine kernels

Marmalade-Glazed Carrots   vf

Melt the butter and sugar together gently in a saucepan, then add all the remaining ingredients. Bring to the boil, and cook uncovered for about 10 minutes until the carrots are tender and the liquid has cooked down to a glaze.

If the liquid has not cooked down enough by the time the carrots are done (depending on the thickness of the carrots and the preferred level of tenderness), either quick-boil off the rest of the liquid, or thicken the sauce with 1 tsp of cornflour-and-water paste.

This dish can be cooked ahead of time and reheated in the saucepan, provided that you leave a little more liquid than is desired, so you have something to heat the mixture with.

Steamed Brussels Sprouts   vf

Peel the outer leaves from the sprouts and cut a cross in each stem. Then simply steam the vegetables until they are tender, and sprinkle the pine kernels over them before serving.

Glazed Parsnips vf

Chop the parsnips into wedges and put into a heavy-bottomed saucepan. Add all the other ingredients except the parsley and stir them together. Cover and simmer, stirring occasionally, for approximately 20 minutes, or until the parsnips are tender and the liquid has reduced to a syrupy glaze. Before serving, sprinkle liberally with the parsley.

Ingredients

700g/1½lb small parsnips, peeled
1 tbsp soft brown sugar
175ml/6fl oz water or vegetable stock
2 tbsp butter or margarine
freshly ground black pepper to taste
good pinch of sea salt
freshly chopped parsley

Ratatouille vf

This very low-fat variation of the classic ratatouille recipe doesn't have any olive oil in it. For a more authentic, tastier, but higher-fat version, add some olive oil with the other ingredients.

For this very simple recipe, just put all ingredients into a large saucepan, bring to the boil and simmer for about 20 minutes. If too much liquid remains, reduce by boiling briskly for a few minutes with the lid off. Remove the bay leaves before serving.

Ingredients

225g/8oz courgettes, scrubbed and
    sliced
2 aubergines, scrubbed and diced
1 large green pepper, de-seeded and
    cut into 15mm/½"-thick cubes
400g/14oz tin chopped tomatoes,
    including juice
2 bay leaves
2 small onions, peeled and finely sliced
1 clove garlic, peeled and finely
    chopped
salt and freshly ground black pepper

Ingredients

450g/1lb carrots, scrubbed and thinly
    sliced
450g/1lb apples, peeled and thinly
    sliced
2 onions, peeled and finely sliced
2 tbsp olive oil
salt and pepper
1 tbsp sugar (optional)

Ingredients

2 small red eating apples, washed and
    cut into bite-sized pieces
juice of 1 lemon
2 sticks of celery, scrubbed and thinly
    sliced
100–125g/4oz chopped walnuts
100–125g/4oz sweet green seedless
    grapes
2 tbsp yoghurt
2 tbsp mayonnaise

Apple and Carrot Surprise   v

An unusual and tasty dish, which can be served hot or cold.

Cook the carrots in a little boiling, salted water until they're nearly tender, then drain, reserving the cooking liquid. Add the apple to the carrots in the saucepan, together with 4 tbsp of the cooking liquid. Cook over a gentle heat, with a lid on the saucepan, for 5–7 minutes or until the apple has reduced to a soft pulp. Fry the onions in the oil until they're crisp and beginning to brown.

Season the apple and carrot mixture with the salt, pepper and sugar to taste. Then serve the dish with the fried onion spooned over the top.

Waldorf and Grape Salad

A variation on the classic Waldorf salad.

Simply mix all the ingredients together.

Spicy Red Cabbage   vf

This classic dish is tasty and colourful, and can be prepared in advance to make for easy entertaining.

Gently fry the onion and cabbage in the oil for about 10 minutes. Add all the other ingredients and mix well, adding enough of your chosen liquid to cover all the ingredients. Cover the pan, and simmer over a low heat for about 1 hour. Finally, remove the cloves and the bay leaf before serving.

Ingredients

1 onion, peeled and sliced
450g/1lb red cabbage, shredded
3 tbsp vegetable oil
1 cooking apple, scrubbed and diced
1 tbsp cider vinegar
1 tbsp demerara sugar
2 cloves
1 bay leaf
pinch of mixed spices
salt
liquid: either cider or red wine mixed with water, or water alone

Cauliflower Salad

This is a lovely summery salad.

If necessary, cut the cauliflower florets into bite-sized pieces. Mix together the remainder of the ingredients except for the parsley. Finally, coat the cauliflower in the dressing, and sprinkle with the parsley to garnish.

Ingredients

1 small cauliflower, separated into small florets
100–125ml/4fl oz mayonnaise, or yoghurt, or a mixture
salt and pepper to taste
1 tbsp lemon juice
1 tbsp fresh parsley, washed and finely chopped

Ingredients

1 onion, peeled and finely chopped
1 clove garlic, peeled and finely chopped
3 tbsp olive oil
3 large tomatoes, skinned and finely
    chopped
½ tbsp mixed herbs
salt and freshly ground black pepper
900g/2lb runner beans, washed,
    topped, and tailed
1 tbsp fresh parsley, washed and finely
    chopped

Ingredients

450g/1lb Brussels sprouts
½ lemon
4 tbsp sunflower oil
1–2 cloves garlic, peeled and finely
    chopped
salt to taste

Runner Beans in Tomato Sauce   vf

You can use French beans for this dish if you prefer. In this case just top and tail them — they are small enough not to need slicing.

Gently fry the onion and garlic in the oil for about 10 minutes until soft. Stir in the tomatoes, mixed herbs, salt and pepper. Cut the beans into thin strips, and cook in salted boiling water for 10–15 minutes until tender. Drain well and stir into the tomato mixture.

Sprinkle with the parsley before serving.

Stir-Fried Sprouts   v

This dish is best cooked just before serving. If you have a food processor you should slice the sprouts just before cooking to keep the nutrients. Otherwise you can slice them in advance, but don't cook them until you are almost ready to serve.

Trim and wash the sprouts, then slice thinly — this is best done in a food processor, and the sprouts should then 'shred'. Zest and juice the lemon, reserving both. In a wok, heat the oil until 'smoky' hot, then add the sprouts, garlic and lemon zest, and stir-fry for 2–3 minutes.

Finally, add the lemon juice and salt, and turn for another minute before serving immediately.

Sweet and Sour Cabbage v

This unusual and substantial dish is very quick to cook, and very nutritious because its short cooking time means that most of the vitamins and minerals are retained.

Gently fry all the vegetables in a wok or frying-pan for 10 minutes. Then blend all the other ingredients together, add to the vegetables, and cook for a further 2–3 minutes.

Ingredients

½ white cabbage, shredded
1 medium carrot, scrubbed, finely sliced
1 small green pepper, de-seeded and
    cut into 15mm/½" squares
1 onion, peeled and thinly sliced
1 clove garlic, peeled and finely chopped
25ml/1fl oz sunflower oil
1 tbsp cider vinegar
100–125ml/4fl oz water
1 tbsp honey or golden syrup
freshly ground pepper
1 tbsp soya sauce
½ tsp sea salt
1 pinch paprika
1 tsp cornflour

Creamy Mashed Potato

Cook the potatoes in plenty of boiling, salted water until they are tender, then drain. Mash the potatoes roughly. Add the butter, cream, and seasoning. Whisk well with an electric whisk until the potatoes are light and fluffy.

You can pipe this mixture into rosettes, and bake at 180°C/350°F/gas mark 4 for about 15 minutes until they are crisp and brown.

Ingredients

900g/2lb potatoes, peeled and cut into
    smallish pieces
50g/2oz butter
100–125ml/4fl oz cream
salt and pepper to taste

Potato Cakes vf

Ingredients

450g/1lb potatoes, scrubbed and
coarsely grated
225g/8oz onions, peeled and finely
chopped
75g/3oz wholemeal flour
salt and pepper to taste
75g/3oz margarine

This dish, which is halfway between the traditional Irish potato cakes and Swiss rosti, makes an unusual accompaniment to a nut roast, roulade, or any other dry main course. To freeze, make the potato cakes up, then freeze uncovered and put into a freezer bag when solid. Defrost before frying.

Put the potatoes, onions, flour, salt and pepper into a mixing bowl and mix well. Melt 50g/2oz of the margarine in a frying-pan over a low heat. Then, using a tablespoon, drop the mixture one spoon at a time into the pan, flattening the cakes with a spatula. Fry several cakes at a time, turning once to brown both sides.

Can be eaten hot or cold.

Rosemary Roast Potatoes v

Ingredients

100–125ml/4fl oz sunflower oil
900g/2lb potatoes
olive oil
rosemary sprigs
salt

Pour the sunflower oil into a large roasting tin and place it in a hot oven. Peel and halve or quarter the potatoes until they are approximately egg-sized, then boil or steam them for about 5 minutes before draining. 'Shake' the potatoes in the saucepan to roughen up the edges, then take the roasting tin out of the oven and put the potatoes into it. Brush the olive oil over the potatoes with a pastry brush, and sprinkle them with rosemary and salt. Bake for about an hour at 210–220°C/425°F/gas mark 7, basting occasionally.

Scalloped Potatoes vf

A tasty and nutritious side dish, which would go well with Ratatouille (see p. 97) or any vegetable stew. It is also lovely with just a green salad, as a light lunch. It can be prepared in advance and just popped in the oven an hour before you want to eat.

Arrange a layer of potatoes on the bottom of a greased ovenproof dish. Sprinkle with some seasoning and a little flour, and dot with margarine. Repeat the layers until all the ingredients have been used, then pour the milk over the top.

Bake in the oven at 190°C/375°F/gas mark 5 for 40 minutes. Sprinkle the cheese and breadcrumbs on top, and bake for a further 20 minutes until the potatoes are tender and the top is crisp and brown.

Ingredients

450g/1lb potatoes, scrubbed and
   thinly sliced
salt and freshly ground black pepper
2 tbsp flour
50g/2oz margarine
150ml/5fl oz milk or soya milk
50g/2oz vegetarian cheese, grated
   (optional)
50g/2oz wholemeal breadcrumbs
   (optional)

Butter Bean Salad v

This is a nice, high-protein salad.

Mix together the beans, tomatoes, scallions and parsley, then whisk the juice, rind, oil and salt together, before pouring over the salad. Mix all the ingredients thoroughly so that they are coated in the oil before serving.

Ingredients

200g/7oz butter beans, cooked (see
   p. 32), or a tin of beans, 200g/7oz
   drained weight
3 large tomatoes, finely chopped
4 scallions, finely chopped
2 tbsp parsley, finely chopped
1 tbsp lemon juice
grated rind of ½ lemon
2 tbsp olive oil or sunflower oil
salt to taste

Ingredients

325–350g/12oz bulgar wheat
boiling water
100–125g/4oz parsley, washed and
    finely chopped
2 tbsp chopped mint, washed and
    finely chopped
2 tbsp scallions, finely chopped
3 tomatoes, finely chopped
2 tbsp lemon juice
5 tbsp olive oil or sunflower oil
salt and freshly ground pepper

Ingredients

100–125g/4oz button mushrooms,
    wiped and thinly sliced
4 tbsp French dressing
50g/4oz spinach, washed and finely
    sliced (discarding the tough central
    stalk)

Tabouleh   v

This classic Middle-Eastern dish is extremely nutritious — the bulgar contains protein and iron, and parsley is full of iron. Parsley doesn't usually contribute much iron to our diet, as we eat it in only small quantities, but the large amount used in this dish makes it a very valuable source of this mineral. Tabouleh travels very well for picnics.

Cover the bulgar wheat with boiling water to a depth of about an inch, and leave for approximately 20 minutes, to cook. Taste a few grains to see if they are cooked — if they are crunchy they need to be left a little longer. When the bulgar is ready, add all the remaining ingredients, mixing well so that they are all combined. Leave the tabouleh for about 15 minutes before serving, to allow the flavours to develop.

Mushroom and Spinach Salad   v

Although not very nutritious, mushrooms are used a lot in vegetarian cookery for their wonderful texture. As well as using button mushrooms, you could use some of the other mushrooms now widely available. Spinach contains useful amounts of iron, together with calcium and many other vitamins and minerals. It is best used raw, as cooking spinach renders these nutrients unusable by the body.

Place the mushrooms in a bowl with the dressing, stir well and leave for about an hour (this 'cooks' the mushrooms, extracting their juices). Add the spinach and stir well, adding more dressing if you wish.

Bread and Pastry

Ingredients

For two loaves
325–350g/12oz good strong white
    bread flour
575g/1lb 4oz good-quality coarse
    wholewheat flour
7 tsp baking powder
pinch of salt
850ml/30fl oz cold water
1 tbsp olive oil

This is the easiest bread that you will ever make. It does not give you indigestion if eaten hot and it freezes well. Slice it before freezing, and just take it out as you want it. The recipe was given to us by Ita West, proprietor of Cussens Cottage, that wonderful vegetarian B&B in Kilmallock, Co. Limerick. According to Ita, she had always made vegan yeast bread until she had some guests who ate only a vegan, macrobiotic diet, which meant that both buttermilk and yeast were out, so she corrupted a soda bread recipe until it worked without the buttermilk. Now she uses nothing else.

Heat the oven to 200°C/400°F/gas mark 6. Use greaseproof paper to line 2 x 900g/2lb loaf tins. Combine the flours, baking powder and salt in the bowl of a food mixer.

Add the water and the oil, using the food processor on the minimum setting for 3 minutes. Stop the machine and make sure that the flour and water are mixed well. Turn the processor to the second setting and mix for another 3 minutes. Pour the mixture (it should be very runny) into the two prepared bread tins. Bake for 55 minutes in the middle of the oven.

The loaves are cooked when they have a hollow sound when tapped on the bottom. Cover with a clean, damp tea towel and leave to cool on a wire tray.

Basic Bread Recipe vf

Bread-making is easy once you get the hang of it, especially if you use the Easy-Blend yeast recommended here. To knead, lift the end of dough furthest from you, and fold it into the middle. Give the dough a quarter turn, and repeat. Make sure the surface you are kneading on is low enough that you can put your whole weight behind it. Most food processors have a dough blade, which will knead your bread in about 30 seconds — however, usually you can make only 450g/1lb of bread at a time.

Place the flour in a large bowl. Add the salt, oil and yeast, and mix. Add the water and mix it through, then place the mixture on a lightly floured surface and knead well for 10 minutes, or until it is smooth and elastic. Either brush with oil and cover loosely with cling film, or cover with a damp tea towel. Leave to double in size — dough will rise at any temperature, even in the fridge. But the warmer its location, the quicker it will rise. If you put it on top of the oven while the oven is warming, or beside a radiator, it should take about an hour. Divide into two and place each half in a 450g/1lb greased loaf tin. Bake at 230°C/450°F/gas mark 8 for about 30 minutes, or until the bread sounds hollow when the bottom is tapped.

If desired, sprinkle sesame, poppy, or sunflower seeds on top of the bread before cooking.

To make pitta bread, take small pieces of the bread dough and roll into very thin ovals. Bake at 230°C/450°F/gas mark 8 for 6–8 minutes. You can also make rolls (cook for about 20 minutes each), and freeze them.

Ingredients

700g/1½lb strong flour, either white, or wholemeal, or a mixture
2 tsp salt
1–2 tbsp olive oil (optional)
1 sachet dried 'Easy Blend' yeast
450ml/15fl oz warm water *

*   To get water of the perfect temperature, use $\frac{1}{3}$ boiling water and $\frac{2}{3}$ cold water, in this case 150ml/5fl oz boiling and 275–300ml/10fl oz cold.

Ingredients

175g/6oz wholemeal flour
50g/2oz strong white flour
2 tsp baking powder
salt (optional)
50g/2oz fat (soya spread)
boiling water to mix

When making pastry with non-dairy fats or oil-based fats, the quantity of fat to flour is much lower than the usual 2:1 ratio. Note that wholemeal pastry is not as easy to handle as white, but if it tears, you can just press the pieces together in the pie dish.

Place all the dry ingredients in the mixing bowl of a food processor (obviously this can also be done by hand). Set at number 3 using the pastry setting, and mix the dry ingredients for about 3 minutes. Add the soya spread in teaspoon-sized lumps. Continue mixing until the mixture resembles breadcrumbs.

Gently add the boiling water from the kettle. Keep pouring slowly, stopping frequently to check the consistency of the pastry. Enough water has been added when the pastry is of a consistency that you can handle, and is not sticky. If the pastry becomes sticky, add flour to correct the consistency.

Roll out the pastry and use straightaway. An average pie cooks in 25 minutes at 200°C/400°F/gas mark 6. Brush the top with soya milk to add a glaze.

Sauces

Sauces can really make a meal, and although there are plenty of packet sauces available, it's cheaper, tastier and healthier to make your own — and they're not difficult, as these recipes will show. All of these sauces can be made ahead of time and reheated (except of course the Mint and Yoghurt Sauce, which is served cold).

Ingredients

1 small carton plain dairy or soya
   yoghurt
1 tsp lemon juice
2½ tsp fresh mint, washed and finely
   chopped
1½ tsp fresh parsley, washed and
   finely chopped
1 small clove garlic, peeled and finely
   chopped

Ingredients

1 dsp cornflour
150ml/5fl oz milk or soya milk
25g/1oz margarine or butter
½ tsp yeast extract
salt and pepper to taste
50g/2oz strong vegetarian cheddar
   cheese, grated
chopped parsley (optional)

Mint and Yoghurt Sauce   v

This refreshing sauce can be served with all burgers, rissoles and nut roasts — it goes especially well with anything that has Indian spices in it.

Simply mix all the ingredients together in a bowl.

Cheese Sauce   f

Mustard goes very well with cheese, bringing out its flavour. So a variation on this dish would be to add 1 tbsp of grain mustard, or 1 tsp of mustard powder. This sauce is brilliant with pasta and cauliflower or broccoli.

Mix the cornflour with about 3 tbsp of the milk until a paste is formed. Melt the butter in a small saucepan. Add to the pan the rest of the milk, the yeast extract, salt and pepper, and simmer gently. Stir in the cornflour paste, and keep stirring until the sauce has thickened. Finally, add the grated cheese and stir until it has melted, sprinkling in the parsley if you're using it.

Mushroom and Sherry Sauce vf

Ingredients

If you prefer to omit the sherry, or if you are vegan, add some herbs such as thyme to give it a different flavour.

Melt the butter in a saucepan and add the mushrooms and sherry (or herbs). Cover the pan, and cook for 3 minutes on a high heat. Remove the pan lid and continue to cook, stirring constantly, until all the liquid has evaporated and the mushrooms are well browned.

Reduce the heat and add the flour gradually, stirring it in well, then cook for 5 minutes more, stirring all the time. Pour in the stock a little at a time, stirring constantly to prevent lumps forming, then simmer the mixture for approximately 4 minutes. Add the seasoning, and leave the sauce to cool a little before putting it in a blender or liquidiser until it is smooth.

25g/1oz butter
225g/8oz mushrooms, quartered
1 tbsp sherry (optional)
3 tsp flour, heaped
575–600ml/1 pint strong vegetable
  stock
salt and freshly ground black pepper
  to taste

Red Pepper Sauce v

Ingredients

A vibrantly coloured sauce, which would go very well with the Spinach Roulade on p. 90. As a variation, try using different-coloured peppers, depending on the colour of the dish you want to serve it with — although it should be said that red peppers are definitely the sweetest, as they are the ripest.

Cook the red peppers with the onion in the stock until soft, then drain. Place the mixture in a blender or food processor with the cream or milk, and blend until it is smooth.

2 red peppers, de-seeded and finely
  chopped
1 onion, peeled and finely chopped
50ml/2fl oz vegetable stock
150ml/5fl oz sour or fresh cream, or
  soya milk

Ingredients

1 small onion, peeled and finely chopped
50g/2oz olive oil
900g/2lb fresh or tinned tomatoes,
    roughly chopped
1 small red pepper, de-seeded and
    finely chopped
3 cloves garlic, peeled and finely chopped
1 bay leaf
2 tsp mixed herbs
salt and pepper to taste

Ingredients

1 small onion, peeled and chopped
1 tbsp vegetable oil
25g/1oz wholemeal or plain flour
425ml/15fl oz water
1 tbsp tomato purée
1 tsp soya sauce
1 clove garlic, peeled and finely chopped
1 tsp yeast extract
1 vegan stock cube
salt and pepper

Tomato Sauce   vf

This classic sauce is great with pasta, nut roasts, burgers, and any vegetable, and can also be used as a pizza topping (see p. 54). Experiment with flavourings too, such as oregano and basil (you can use some pesto sauce for the basil) — both go very well with tomatoes, and are classics in Italian cooking. If you are using fresh tomatoes, skin them by placing them for a minute in a saucepan of boiled water. As this sauce freezes so well, and is used in so many dishes, it's worthwhile batch-cooking and freezing it.

Gently fry the onion in the oil for about 10 minutes, or until soft. Add the tomatoes, red pepper and garlic, and stir well. Simmer for 10 minutes. Add the herbs, salt and pepper, and simmer for another 10 minutes. Remove the bay leaf before serving.

Vegetarian Gravy   vf

Most traditional gravy has a meat base, so is obviously unsuitable for vegetarians — here's one that's as rich and savoury as you'll get, and is handy for so many dishes.

Fry the onion in the oil for 10 minutes on a low heat. Add the flour and let it brown over the heat, stirring all the time. Put in all the remaining ingredients and bring to the boil, then simmer for 10 minutes, stirring occasionally. Season to taste.

You can liquidise this gravy if you prefer.

112

Spreads and Pâtés

Dips, pâtés and spreads are an essential ingredient in our lives today. Serve these dishes as dips with strips of pitta bread, wholemeal toast or vegetable crudités. Or you can use them as sandwich fillings, perhaps with some salad, or you can pipe the spreads decoratively onto savoury biscuits for a party.

If some of these dishes seem high in fat, it's because they are! You can do one of two things — either reduce the amount of oil used, or console yourself with the thought that traditional meat pâtés are among the highest-fat foods you'll find.

Ingredients

1 large aubergine
1 small clove garlic, peeled and finely
    chopped
juice of 1 lemon
salt and freshly ground black pepper
50g/2fl oz olive oil
2 tbsp tahini
4 or 5 black olives, stoned and
    roughly chopped
parsley, washed and finely chopped

Aubergine Pâté   v

This traditional Turkish pâté is quite strong-tasting and can be a bit of an acquired taste.

Prick the aubergine, then cook in one of the following ways:

- Grill under high heat, turning frequently, or
- Bake at 190°C/375°F/gas mark 5, for approximately 1 hour, or
- Cover with kitchen paper and microwave for about 6 minutes, or
- Barbecue (this is the authentic method, giving a distinctive taste).

When the skin is black and the aubergine has collapsed and gone saggy, it's cooked. Leave aside to cool, then peel off the burnt skin, and chop the flesh coarsely into a bowl (or into a food processor or blender). Add the garlic and the juice of the lemon, and season to taste. Beat well until smooth (or process, if you are using a machine).

Gradually mix in the olive oil, making sure it's completely absorbed, then stir in the tahini to make a thick, smooth mixture. Finally, sprinkle with the olives and parsley before serving.

Hummus  vf

Another classic dip from the Middle East, hummus is extremely nutritious, being high in protein and calcium. The traditional way of serving it is to put it on a flat plate, drag a fork over it to form ridges and valleys, then pour olive oil over it and sprinkle olives and paprika on top. It is traditionally eaten with fingers of pitta bread, but crudités are good too. If you use less water to make a thicker purée it can be used as a pâté or sandwich spread. It will freeze for up to two weeks.

Put the chick-peas, garlic, olive oil, tahini, lemon juice and paprika into a food processor or blender, and process, adding the stock to form a thick purée. Season to taste.

Ingredients

225g/8oz cooked chick-peas, or 1 tin chick-peas, 225g/8oz drained weight
1 garlic clove, peeled and finely chopped
1 tbsp olive oil
2 tbsp tahini
1 tbsp lemon juice
1 tsp paprika
100–125ml/4fl oz chick-pea stock, or water
salt and pepper

Ingredients

3 tbsp margarine
1 onion, peeled and finely chopped
1 tsp marjoram
225g/8oz red lentils
425ml/15fl oz vegetable stock or
    water
50g/2oz wholewheat breadcrumbs
salt and freshly ground black pepper

Lentil Spread

vf

A handy sandwich spread. You could add some garlic to the recipe if you wish.

Melt the margarine in a saucepan, and gently fry the onion with the marjoram for about 10 minutes or until soft. Add the lentils and the stock, bring to the boil, then simmer gently with the lid on until the lentils are soft and all the liquid is absorbed (about 20 minutes).

Stir in the breadcrumbs, salt and pepper, then place in a bowl and leave to cool before using.

Red Pepper Pâté   v

This delicious pâté doesn't keep very well because of the tofu. If you want to make it vegan, replace the mayonnaise with an extra 2 tbsp of olive oil.

Marinate the red pepper in the olive oil for as long as is handy — ideally 2 hours. Put the peppers (including all the olive oil), the lemon juice and the mayonnaise into a food processor or blender, and process for about 1 minute. Add the water and blend for 30 seconds more, then add half the tofu and blend for a further minute. Finally, add the remaining tofu and the seasonings, and blend until it is creamy.

Ingredients

1 large red pepper, de-seeded and
    chopped
2 tbsp olive oil
2 tbsp lemon juice
2 tbsp mayonnaise
2 tbsp water
225g/8oz tofu, roughly chopped
salt and pepper to taste

Ingredients

225g/8oz dried apricots
pure apple juice
1 tbsp arrowroot or cornflour
275–300ml/10fl oz orange juice
tiny pinch of salt
1½ tsp grated orange rind

Ingredients

40g/1½oz dried dates
6 tbsp water
175g/6oz cashew nuts, finely ground
3 tsp carob powder
1½ tbsp vegetable oil

Apricot and Orange Spread v

Put the apricots into a pan with enough apple juice to cover the fruit. Simmer until the apricots are soft (about 10 minutes), then purée them in a blender or chop them finely.

Put the arrowroot or cornflour into a saucepan with the orange juice and bring to the boil, stirring all the time, until the mixture thickens. Add the apricot purée, salt, and orange rind to this, and simmer for 1–2 minutes more. Leave to cool before serving.

Cashew and Date Spread v

Cook the dates in the water over a low heat until they are soft. Remove from the heat and place in a food processor or blender with all the remaining ingredients. Process until you have a smooth spread.

*Both recipes on this page are for sweet spreads,
which can be used like jam on bread or toast.*

Cakes and Desserts

Cakes and desserts can be full of nutrition if you use good ingredients such as those used in the following recipes. The only thing to be careful of is that they tend to be high in fat, but they are fine as part of a balanced diet.

Ingredients

100–125g/4oz butter or margarine
50g/2oz carob drops
2 free-range eggs
225g/8oz demerara sugar
50g/2oz wholemeal flour, sifted
½ tsp vanilla essence
50g/2oz walnuts, roughly chopped
icing sugar for dredging

When you sift wholemeal flour, you'll be left with the bran in the sieve — simply tip this into the bowl. The idea behind sifting is to lighten and aerate the flour, not to remove the bran.

Line a 20cm/8"-square shallow baking tin with greaseproof paper and grease the paper well with margarine.

Gently melt the butter and carob together in a bowl over a saucepan of boiling water — or you can do this in the microwave (see note in glossary). Whisk the eggs with the sugar until the mixture is thick and pale, and fold the carob and butter mixture into this.

Add the flour, vanilla and nuts, mixing gently but thoroughly, then pour the mixture into the prepared tin. Bake for 40–45 minutes at 180°C/350°F/gas mark 4, or until the centre has set. (Take care not to over-bake, as the inside should still be gooey.) Leave to cool in the tin, then dredge with icing sugar. Finally, cut the brownies into squares and remove from the tin to serve.

Courgette Cake f

Carrot cake is something we are all used to. Here's a novel idea using courgettes! This cake is lovely with tea or coffee, or can be served in squares with soya or dairy cream as a dessert.

Simply mix all the ingredients together thoroughly in a large bowl. Then divide the mixture between 2 x 900g/2lb loaf tins and bake at 180°C/ 350°F/gas mark 4 for 1 hour. Leave to cool for 10 minutes, then loosen with a knife and carefully remove from the tins before placing on a wire cooling rack.

Ingredients

225g/8oz plain or wholemeal flour
225g/8oz sugar
100–125g/4oz chopped walnuts
1 tbsp baking powder
1 tsp mixed spice
½ tsp salt
3 free-range eggs, beaten
150ml/5fl oz sunflower oil
225g/8oz grated courgette
1 tsp grated lemon rind

Carob and Banana Sponge vf

If you don't have any self-raising flour, use plain flour and an extra 2 tsp baking powder. A nice variation on this cake is to mash the bananas through the cake mixture. As with the Courgette Cake, this is also nice served as dessert with cream.

Sift the flour, carob, and baking powder into a bowl, then add the sugar and the remaining ingredients except for the bananas. Mix to a smooth consistency. Peel and slice the bananas, and place the slices on the bottom of a lined 25cm/10" baking tin. Pour the mixture on top.

Bake the sponge at 190°C/375°F/gas mark 5 for 25–30 minutes. Turn out upside down so the bananas are on top. Leave to cool on a wire rack.

Ingredients

100–125g/4oz self-raising flour
2 tbsp carob powder
2 tsp baking powder
175g/6oz soft brown sugar
6 tbsp sunflower oil
200ml/7fl oz water
½ tsp vanilla essence
2 bananas

Ingredients

100–125g/4oz carob drops (or
cooking chocolate)
4 free-range eggs, separated
optional flavourings: peppermint
essence, or liqueur such as
Cointreau or kirsch, or whiskey or
brandy, or grated orange rind
whipped cream and/or 4 carob drops,
grated

Carob Mousse

This recipe is lovely as part of a meal for a special occasion, as it is rich enough to be special, but light enough to eat after a heavy meal. Be careful though, as the recipe contains raw eggs, so it should not be eaten if you are pregnant or elderly.

Melt the carob in a bowl over a saucepan of boiling water, or use the defrost setting of the microwave for 5 minutes. Mix the egg yolks into the melted carob. At this stage add your chosen flavouring.

Whisk the egg whites until they are stiff, then fold them gently into the carob/egg-yolk mixture, using a metal spoon. Put the mixture into four decorative bowls or glasses and chill for at least 1 hour. Decorate with the whipped cream and/or grated carob.

Baklava

To make the pastry, put 4 tbsp of the melted butter or margarine into a pan, and add the sugar, water, and nuts. Grease a baking tray large enough to take the filo pastry (or cut the pastry to fit your tin). Lay three sheets of the pastry in the bottom, brushing each sheet with melted butter. Spread a thin layer of the nut mixture on top, then sprinkle with a little cinnamon, and cover with two more sheets of pastry (brushing each sheet with melted butter). Keep repeating these layers, finishing with a top layer of filo pastry three sheets deep. Finally, brush the top with melted butter and score with a sharp knife into a diamond pattern. Bake at 190°C/375°F/gas mark 5 for about 30 minutes until golden brown.

When the pastry is nearly ready, make the syrup. Boil the sugar, honey or golden syrup, water and lemon juice together for about 5 minutes. Allow the mixture to cool a little before pouring it over the cooked pastry. If possible, leave the baklava for a day before eating it, to give the syrup time to soak in. This dessert is particularly nice served with cream.

Ingredients

butter or margarine, melted
225g/8oz sugar
225ml/8fl oz hot water
275g/10oz ground or chopped nuts,
   e.g. almonds and/or walnuts
300g/11oz packet filo pastry (use
   brand made with vegetable fat)
1 tbsp ground cinnamon

For the syrup
225g/8oz sugar
325–350ml/12fl oz honey or golden
   syrup
225ml/8fl oz water
juice of 1 lemon

Ingredients

50g/2oz dried figs
50g/2oz dried banana
50g/2oz dried apricots
175g/6oz dried dates
25g/1oz margarine
50g/2oz ground almonds
50g/2oz ground coconut

Ingredients

100–125g/4oz unsalted cashew nuts
100–125g/4oz plain vegetarian cottage
    cheese
1 tbsp honey, or less if preferred
150ml/5fl oz water or milk

Fruit Chews   V

All the dried fruit in this recipe makes for a very nutritious cake which children love. It is also so simple that children can make it themselves (with a little parental help and supervision).

Chop the dried fruit finely, preferably in a food processor. Melt the margarine in a saucepan over a low heat, then add the fruit and stir for a few minutes until soft. Add the nuts and coconut, mixing well, then turn the mixture onto a well-greased baking tray and flatten with the back of a spoon.

When cool, cut into fingers, and put in the fridge to chill.

Cashew Nut Cream

This is a cream substitute, but it is not dairy-free. It goes particularly well with the Sugar-Free Mincemeat pies and the Christmas Pudding (see pp. 127 and 126).

Simply blend all the ingredients in a liquidiser until the mixture is smooth.

Drain the peaches, keeping the juice, and leave the fruit to one side. Add water to the juice to make up one pint, then place the water/peach-juice mixture and sugar into a saucepan, and heat, stirring, until the sugar dissolves.

Add the honey or syrup, cinnamon, nutmeg, cloves, lemon juice and brandy, and bring to the boil. Reduce the heat, then add the apricots, cover and simmer for 15 minutes. Stir in the peaches and simmer for 30 minutes more. Remove the cloves and add the sultanas just before serving.

Serve hot with whipped cream or Greek-style yoghurt.

Ingredients

2 x 400g/14oz tins peaches in fruit juice
25g/1oz soft brown sugar
1 tbsp clear honey
1 tsp ground cinnamon
1 tsp nutmeg
3 cloves
2 tbsp lemon juice
1 tbsp brandy (optional)
100–125g/4oz dried apricots
50g/2oz sultanas
whipped cream or Greek-style yoghurt (optional)

Ingredients

325–350g/12oz mixed dried fruit
50g/2oz demerara sugar
225ml/8fl oz apple juice
2 medium carrots, grated
1 red apple, grated
75g/3oz wheat-free vegetarian suet
6 rice cakes, crushed
100g/4oz rice flour
½ tsp wheat-free baking powder
1 tsp mixed spice
½ tsp nutmeg

Christmas Pudding

Serves eight

For a truly festive pudding you can substitute up to half the apple juice for the same quantity of rum. The recipe caters for those who are allergic to wheat, but if you are not, you can use ordinary vegetarian suet and baking powder.

Put the dried fruit into a mixing bowl with the sugar and apple juice, and soak for at least 2 hours. Add the carrots, apple and suet, and mix well.

Crush the rice cakes in a grinder or food processor until they resemble coarse breadcrumbs. Add to the mixing bowl along with the rice flour, baking powder and spices, and mix thoroughly. Spoon the mixture into a greased 1.15-litre/2-pint pudding basin and smooth the surface with a spatula. Using a sheet of parchment or greaseproof paper, make a double fold down the middle to form a pleat. Use this to cover the basin and allow for expansion. Cover with a sheet of foil tied in place with string.

Stand the basin on a trivet in a large pan, and add boiling water to come two-thirds of the way up the side of the basin. Cover and steam over a low heat for about 3½ hours, topping up with boiling water as required. Lift the basin carefully from the water and leave to cool. Wrap in fresh parchment and foil and store in a cool place (do not freeze).

To reheat, steam for 1½ hours; or, to reheat in a microwave (using a plastic basin), remove the wrappings and cover the basin with microwave cling film, being sure to pierce the film. Cook on full power for 3–4 minutes and allow to stand for 5 minutes before serving.

Sugar-Free Mincemeat vf

Fills 4 x 325–350g/12oz jars

Ingredients

Put the apples, dried fruit and apple juice into a saucepan and cover. Bring to the boil, then simmer for 30 minutes. Add a small amount of liquid from the pan to the miso, mix well, then put back into the pan. Stir in the lemon rind, brandy and spices, then leave to cool. Let the mincemeat stand for a day or two in the refrigerator before using.

Spoon the mincemeat into clean, sterilised* jars and cover, then keep stored in the refrigerator until needed. This recipe will keep for two or three weeks.

To make mince pies, use your usual pastry recipe, or buy ready-made frozen vegetable-fat pastry and follow the baking instructions on the packet. If you want to make these ahead of time, make them as usual but cook for about 5 minutes less, then freeze. Bake for about 15 minutes from frozen.

* To sterilise jars, wash them well and dry them, then place in an oven at 130°C/250°F/gas mark ½ for about 15 minutes.

700g/1½lb eating apples, peeled, cored and grated
450g/1lb mixed dried fruits, e.g. raisins, sultanas, apricots, currants
275–300ml/10fl oz natural unsweetened apple juice
1 tbsp miso
grated rind of 1 lemon
2 tbsp brandy
1 tsp ground cinnamon
1 tsp mixed spice
½ tsp ground ginger

Ingredients

75g/3oz butter
1 tbsp black treacle
100–125g/4oz demerara sugar
½ tsp ground nutmeg
½ tsp ground cinnamon
2 tsp ground ginger
pinch of ground cloves
450g/1lb strong white plain flour
1½ tsp baking powder
pinch of salt
2 free-range eggs, beaten

Makes approximately forty biscuits

Melt the butter in a heavy-bottomed saucepan over a low heat, then add the treacle, sugar and spices. Stir until the sugar dissolves, then leave to cool. Sieve the flour, baking powder and salt into a mixing bowl and make a well in the centre. Pour the beaten eggs and the cool treacle mixture into the well, and stir very carefully from the centre to mix in the flour gradually.

Turn the mixture out onto a lightly floured board and knead for a minute or two until it is smooth. Cover the mixture with cling film and leave to rest in the refrigerator for at least 30 minutes. Roll out the dough to 3mm/⅛" thick and cut into assorted shapes. Transfer these to a lightly greased baking sheet and bake for 8–10 minutes at 160–170°C/325°F/gas mark 3. Take care not to bake too long, as these biscuits burn easily. Leave to cool on a wire rack, then store in an airtight container.

Walnut Loaf vf

This simple cake is very nutritious with its wholemeal flour and dates. It is also very low in fat as there's no added fat at all.

Grease a 1lb/450g loaf tin with margarine and line it with greaseproof paper. Simmer the dates in the water until they are soft (about 10 minutes), then mash to form a purée (a potato masher is ideal for this). Allow to cool. Sift the flour and baking powder into a bowl, then add the walnuts, vanilla and date mixture, and stir well.

Spoon into the prepared tin and bake at 180°C/350°F/gas mark 4 for 50–60 minutes. Allow to cool before serving.

Ingredients

175g/6oz dried dates
275–300ml/10fl oz water
175g/6oz plain wholemeal flour
3 tsp baking powder
75g/3oz walnuts, chopped
½ tsp vanilla essence or extract

Coconut Biscuits v

For this easy recipe, simply put all the ingredients into a bowl and mix well. Roll out to about 3mm/¹/₈" thick and cut into squares or rounds. Then place well apart on a greased tin.

Bake for 10 minutes at 180°C/350°F/gas mark 4.

Ingredients

100–125g/4oz wholemeal flour
100–125g/4oz sugar
100–125g/4oz oatmeal
100–125g/4oz margarine, melted
100–125g/4oz desiccated coconut
2 tbsp warm water
1 tbsp golden syrup or barley malt
1 tsp bread soda

Ingredients

200g/7oz wholemeal flour
1 tsp ground ginger
1 tsp baking powder
40g/1½oz butter or margarine
225g/8oz carrots
50g/2oz dark brown sugar
50g/2oz seedless raisins and/or
    sultanas
4 tbsp treacle, or golden syrup, or
    honey
6 tbsp liquid — use one of the
    following: milk, skimmed milk, soya
    milk, or water

Icing (optional)
225g/8oz vegetarian cream cheese
50g/2oz icing sugar
grated rind of 1 orange

Carrot Cake   vf

Ah yes, here's that classic!

Mix the flour with the ginger and baking powder into a bowl, then rub in the fat until the mixture resembles fine breadcrumbs (or whiz in the food processor). Grate the carrots finely (again, the food processor is perfect for this — use the chopping blade), and stir this into the flour mixture along with the sugar and raisins/sultanas. Mix the treacle (or golden syrup or honey) with the milk or water, and add to the flour mixture. If the mixture seems dry, add a little more liquid — it should stick together when pressed, without being sloppy. Stir well, then put into a greased and base-lined loaf tin.

Bake for 45 minutes at 160–170°C/325°F/gas mark 3, or until firm to touch, and golden. Turn out onto a wire rack to cool.

If you are making the icing, simply combine the ingredients well and smooth over the top of the cake.

Jelly v

As gelatine is not suitable for vegetarians, we use a vegetarian gelling agent. The easiest to get and to use is a brand called Vege-Gel. All vegetarian gelling agents are based on seaweeds, which make them a good source of iodine. Some recipes use agar-agar — if you can't get this, adapt the recipes using Vege-Gel.

Put the water and sugar into a saucepan and heat until the sugar has melted. Add the Vege-Gel and bring to the boil, stirring all the time. Simmer for about 5 minutes, still stirring. Add the fruit juice and mix well.

If you are using the fruit pieces, place them in the bottom of an ovenproof glass bowl. Pour the jelly mixture over them and leave to set in the fridge for at least 1 hour.

Ingredients

200ml/7fl oz water
100–125g/4oz sugar — or to taste
3 tsp Vege-Gel
575–600ml/1 pint fruit juice, such as orange or pineapple
pieces of fruit (optional)

Summer Delight

Place alternate spoonfuls of jelly, yoghurt, cottage cheese, fruit and ice-cream into two large or four small sundae dishes. Then simply chill and serve.

Ingredients

1 portion jelly (see Jelly recipe above)
150g/5oz yoghurt, either soya or dairy
100–125g/4oz vegetarian cottage cheese
225g/8oz fresh fruit
50g/2oz ice-cream, either soya or dairy

Ingredients

1 carton soya dessert (Provamel gives
   the best result)
150ml/5fl oz soya milk

Ingredients

275g/10oz short-grain brown rice
700–725ml/25fl oz water
25g/1oz chopped hazelnuts
25g/1oz chopped almonds
100–125g/4oz caster sugar
pinch of nutmeg
50g/2oz raisins
1.5 litres/2½ pints milk or soya milk

Vegan Ice-Cream   vf

This simple dessert is very nice as it is, but if you like, you can add extras such as carob or plain vegan chocolate chips, or nuts and/or fruit, to taste.

Freeze the soya dessert overnight in the freezer or the ice compartment of the refrigerator. When you are ready to make the dessert, peel off the packaging and cut the frozen dessert into cubes. Place in a food processor with the soya milk and blend until smooth. Serve immediately.

Nutty Rice Pudding   vf

This wholefood version of the classic dessert is both very nutritious and very tasty.

Cook the rice in a covered saucepan following the instructions on p. 34. When it is cooked, add all the other ingredients and put into a greased pudding dish. Bake at 180°C/350°F/gas mark 4 for about 20 minutes.

Menus

Christmas Menu I

Recipes by VSI-approved cookery demonstrator Tracy Culleton

Starter
Curried Parsnip Soup — page 38
with
Home-Made Bread Rolls — page 107
(see Basic Bread Recipe)

Main Course
Raised Mushroom and Leek Pie — page 92
with
Spicy Red Cabbage — page 99
Stir-Fried Sprouts — page 100
Creamy Mashed Potatoes — page 101
Marmalade-Glazed Carrots — page 96
and Vegetarian Gravy — page 112

Dessert
Carob Mousse — page 122

Christmas Menu II

Recipes by VSI-approved cookery demonstrator Deirdre Kuntz

Starter
Carrot and Ginger Soup with Sesame Toast — page 39

Main Course
Aubergine and Couscous en Croûte — page 93
with
Glazed Parsnips — page 97
Steamed Brussels Sprouts — page 96
Rosemary Roast Potatoes — page 102
and Mushroom and Sherry Sauce — page 111

Dessert
Hot Spicy Fruit Salad — page 125
followed by
Christmas Pudding — page 126
Cashew Nut Cream — page 124
and
Sugar-Free Mince Pies — page 127

Sunday Dinner

Starter
Apple and White Wine Soup — page 40

Main Course
Red Peppers Stuffed with Almonds — page 50
with broccoli and boiled new potatoes
Mushroom and Spinach Salad — page 104

Dessert
Summer Delight — page 131

Buffet Party

Mini Millet Rissoles — page 81
Mini Pizzas — page 54
Falafel — page 48
Sausage rolls
Mushroom Vol-au-Vents — page 47
Tabouleh — page 104
Green salad
Potato salad
Coleslaw
Carob and Banana Sponge — page 121
served with cream or soya cream

Note:
Make the rissoles and pizzas following the recipes, but
make each one 'nibble-sized'.
A 2" or 3" (5cm or 7.5cm) scone-cutter is ideal for the
pizzas. For the sausage rolls simply use vegetarian
sausage mix, and use with puff pastry exactly as with
sausage-meat rolls. The green salad, potato salad and
coleslaw can be bought or made — recipes are not
given in this book.

Children's Party

Savoury
Potato Cakes — page 102
Mini Pizzas — page 54 (see note on Buffet Party menu)
Sausage Rolls — see note on Buffet Party menu

Sweet
Carob Brownies — page 120
Vegan Ice-Cream — page 132
Jelly — page 131

Greek Meal

Starter
Falafel — page 48

Main Course
Chick-Pea and Apricot Casserole — page 55
Tabouleh — page 104

Dessert
Baklava — page 123

Bibliography

Cox, Peter, *The Realeat Encyclopaedia of Vegetarian Living*, Bloomsbury. (*Recommended if you want further details on the ethics, health studies, and nutrition of vegetarianism. It also gives some lovely recipes at the back. ISBN: 0-7475-2171-9.*)

Elliot, Rose, *Complete Vegetarian Cookbook*, Harper Collins. (*An extremely comprehensive book with recipes that are tasty, healthy and easy. ISBN: 0-00-412711-0.*)

Elliot, Rose, *Mother, Baby and Toddler Book*, Harper Collins. (*Deals with nutrition in pregnancy, breast-feeding and weaning, and gives practical advice for new mums and dads. ISBN: 0-00-412986-5.*)

La Leche League, *The Womanly Art of Breastfeeding*. (*ISBN: 0-912500-25-5.*)

Index

ly Vegetarian